parents have that experience. They would certainly fail if they focused on each specific behavior and possible associated reasons for it and consequences to give. Instead, these authors focus on where we get stuck (our 'knee-jerk reactions' and 'common pitfalls') as well as what we tend to overlook (our child's mind along with our own) and present a way forward—a script that reaches into all manner of situations that are proving to be extra challenging. They show us how to build a bridge to the child's mind, develop possible emotional translations for what we discover in our child, and put our discoveries into practical words that lead our child to feeling understood and being more willing to join us in a way that works for us both.

"Miller and Lafrance suggest possible scripts for a great many situations, while encouraging us parents to adapt them for our unique child and family. As a bonus, they offer scripts that might be of value in bridge-building with our partner too. After all, all family relationships are likely to become tricky and messy. This is a good book to take with us on our journey as we try to 'get it right' as well as to engage in the 'do-overs' that will certainly be necessary. This is a note of gratitude to these authors for their clearly written and oh-so-practical book for parents everywhere."

> – **Dan Hughes, PhD,** founder of Dyadic Developmental Psychotherapy (DDP)
> and author of many books including *Attachment Focused Parenting:*
> *Building the Bonds of Attachment (3rd Ed.)*

"In this wonderful book for parents, Drs. Miller and Lafrance share the fruits of attachment theory and neuroscience to respond to those parenting situations when things get tough. Blending their clinical experience with their own humble and relatable real-life experience as parents and (imperfect) human beings, they remind us that the most precious gift we can offer for children (and ourselves) is our unconditional loving presence. Not satisfied to stop there, they go on to share practical strategies and language that can be applied today, to rebuild and repair the bridge with our children, as well as with ourselves and our co-parent(s)."

> – **Dzung X. Vo, MD,** author of *The Mindful Teen: Powerful Skills to*
> *Help You Handle Stress One Moment at a Time*

"Wisdom is scarce and even common sense is not that common, but both are to be found in abundance in this gem of a book by Miller and Lafrance. Offering both a conceptual framework and practical suggestions, this book provides much needed answers for how to respond supportively and constructively to a wide variety of potentially tricky interactions with children. From day to day interactions, to coping with difficult emotions or tough questions, to handling moments of crisis such as a child who experiences a loss – raising a child can often feel like walking through a minefield. Parents will find that the advice of Miller and Lafrance provides a uniquely effective map for navigating through it. The personal tone, rich vignettes, and charming illustrations make the book especially relatable and easy to read. This is surely one for every parent's bookshelf!"

> – **Eli R. Lebowitz,** associate professor in the Child Study Center,
> Yale School of Medicine

What to Say to Kids When Nothing Seems to Work

What to Say to Kids When Nothing Seems to Work offers parents an effective, step-by-step guide to some of the most common struggles for kids aged 5–12. Written by mental health professionals with over 30 years' experience listening to kids' thoughts and feelings, this book provides a framework to explore new ways of responding to your child that will help them calm down faster and boost their resilience to stress.

With a dose of humor and plenty of real-life examples, the authors will guide you to "build a bridge" into your child's world to make sense of their emotions and behavior. Sample scenarios and scripts are provided for you to customize based on your caregiving style and your child's personality. These are then followed by concrete support strategies to help you manage current and future situations in a way that leaves everyone feeling better. Chapters are organized by common kid-related issues so you can quickly find what's relevant to you.

Suitable for parents, grandparents, and other caregivers of children and pre-teens, as well as professionals working closely with families, *What to Say to Kids When Nothing Seems to Work* is an accessible resource for efficiently navigating the twists, turns, and sometimes total chaos of life with kids.

Adele Lafrance, PhD, is a clinical psychologist, research scientist, and co-developer of Emotion-Focused Family Therapy. She offers workshops for the general public and mental health agencies worldwide.

Ashley Miller, MD, is a child psychiatrist at BC Children's Hospital and a clinical assistant professor of psychiatry at the University of British Columbia where she is co-director of family therapy training for psychiatry residents.

What to Say to Kids When Nothing Seems to Work

A Practical Guide for Parents and Caregivers

ADELE LAFRANCE, PHD AND ASHLEY MILLER, MD

ILLUSTRATIONS BY PATRICK CARLSON

Routledge
Taylor & Francis Group

NEW YORK AND LONDON

First published 2020
by Routledge
52 Vanderbilt Avenue, New York, NY 10017

and by Routledge
2 Park Square, Milton Park, Abingdon, Oxon, OX14 4RN

Routledge is an imprint of the Taylor & Francis Group, an informa business

© 2020 Taylor & Francis

Library of Congress Cataloging-in-Publication Data
Names: Lafrance, Adele, author. | Miller, Ashley P., author.
Title: What to say to kids when nothing seems to work: a practical
    guide for parents and caregivers / Adele Lafrance, PhD
    and Ashley Miller, MD ; illustrations by Patrick Carlson.
Description: New York, NY : Routledge, 2020. | Includes
    bibliographical references and index. |
Identifiers: LCCN 2019046991 (print) | LCCN 2019046992 (ebook) |
Subjects: LCSH: Parent and child. | Child psychology. | Emotions in
    children. | Parenting—Psychological aspects.
Classification: LCC HQ755.85 .L3324 2020 (print) |
    LCC HQ755.85 (ebook) | DDC 306.874—dc23
LC record available at https://lccn.loc.gov/2019046991
LC ebook record available at https://lccn.loc.gov/2019046992

ISBN: 978-1-138-34462-4 (hbk)
ISBN: 978-1-138-34463-1 (pbk)
ISBN: 978-0-429-43839-4 (ebk)

Typeset in Myriad Pro
by Swales & Willis, Exeter, Devon, UK

Dedications

To Lorraine, who showed me that the surest way to help anyone solve their
problems is to first listen deeply.
– AM

To the many parents and caregivers with whom I've had the honor of walking
alongside – you've taught me more than any textbook ever could.
– AL

Contents

Acknowledgments

I would like to start by thanking my children, Noam and Maya, who truly have been my greatest teachers. I'm grateful to my husband, Avri, who has patiently watched me wrestle with what it means to be a "good-enough parent" and who has kept everything functioning while I devoted time to this project. I'd like to thank my parents, Rhoda and Harold Miller, for their unconditional love and support. There are so many people who encouraged me to write and helped me through my doubts. A giant thank you to friends and colleagues: Jessica Morrison, Mark Supino, Cailey Lynch, Alana Hirsh, Melanie Chartier, Jennifer Russel, Muffy Greenaway, Evelyn Stewart, Patricia Frew, Dzung X. Vo, Shimi Kang, Victoria Hurst-Martin, Amrit Dhariwal, Rachel Armstrong, and, of course, my wonderful co-author, Adele Lafrance.

And finally, to my mentors: Dr. E. Jane Garland, who first introduced me to mindfulness practice when I was a new mother, who always knows what I need before I do and who always gifts her complete presence; and Lorraine Hathaway, my greatest role model, whose tremendous attention, empathy, and love have helped raise a whole generation of child psychiatrists, children, and parents. – AM

Thank you to my teachers, mentors, friends, and family members, in particular my step-children. Special thanks to my loving husband John and, of course, my partner in crime, Ashley. This book was so much fun to write and I can't wait for the next one! – AL

Finally (and for real this time!), to everyone at Taylor & Francis: Thank you for believing in this book and supporting us to bring these ideas to a wider audience of clinicians and parents. Sincere gratitude to Elizabeth Budd for her assistance with copyediting. To all the researchers, clinicians, and experts who have come before, we feel so indebted to your contributions for parents and professionals. To our colleagues who have taught us, offered support and helped us along the way – many, many thanks. In these categories, we'd like to formally recognize (in alphabetical order): Jonathon Baylin, Brené Brown, Susan Bogels, Joanne Dolhanty, Adele Faber, John Gottman, Daniel Hughes, Leslie Greenberg, Sue Johnson, Jon and Myla Kabat-Zinn, Gary Landreth, Jay Lebow, Harriet Lerner, Eli Lebowitz, Gabor Maté, Laura Markham, Elaine Mazlish, Kristin Neff, Gordon Neufeld, Gail Palmer, Daniel Siegel, and many, many more. Thanks also to the parents and caregivers who volunteered to review earlier drafts of our manuscripts and who provided invaluable feedback to make it fit better for "real life." – AL & AM

A Note to Our Readers

To write this book, we have drawn on our training and many years practicing as mental health professionals, as well as our own parenting experiences. We have also been informed by our reading of scientific books and articles. This note is to remind readers that ideas and strategies described in this book are general in nature and are not intended as a substitute for medical or psychological treatment. Although we offer some suggested websites and books as resources, we also aren't able to guarantee their content will be appropriate for your situation. All scenarios described in this book are fictional but inspired by real-life events.

Part I

Introduction

A New Path 1

All Rachel wants to do is get out of the house and get some groceries. It's Sunday afternoon, so she'll need to bring the kids along. She already thought ahead and let them know the plan this morning. Ten minutes before it's time to leave, she asks her children, who are 9 and 7 years old, to start getting ready. Five minutes later, she sees her 7-year-old daughter humming to herself while she puts her shoes on. Her 9-year-old son is sitting on the sofa, arms folded across his chest. "I'm not going," he says. Rachel has been here before, so her pulse quickens a bit. "Stay positive," she tells herself silently. She says, "C'mon; it'll be fun. You can choose the kind of cereal you want." Her son is not impressed and digs his heels in further. After a few more attempts to stay calm, Rachel realizes it's not working; her son is stuck in resistance. Rachel decides it's time to take charge with a consequence: "We're leaving. If you don't get up right now, there will be no video games for the rest of the week!" Angrily, he gets up, walks over to his sister and punches her in the arm. She starts wailing and Rachel yells: "That's it, no video games for the week and to your room – now!"

Whaaat just happened?!

Her partner, Jeff, watched the scene unfold from the kitchen. "I would have handled that differently," he thinks. A week later, it's his turn to do groceries with the kids in tow. "Okay, guys, we're leaving in 5 minutes, no ifs, ands, or buts." This time, his son makes some moves toward the door, but then takes his sister's shoe and throws it outside the house. "Dad! He threw my shoe outside!" she cries. "Listen, bud," says Jeff tensely, "You're coming to the store and that's that. Get your sister's shoe and stop fooling around." He throws the shoe in the house, narrowly missing his sister with the toss. "I said stop fooling around!" Jeff yells. "I'm not going to the stupid store, and you can't make me!" the boy yells back and stomps up to his room.

If you've picked up this book, chances are you've had moments with your child when you've felt frustrated, exasperated, or even out of control. Maybe you'd even like to lock yourself in your bedroom with a good book or drop your child off at his grandparents for the month. You're in good company because it happens to us all. Parenting can be hard. Really hard. And there are some common scenarios that stump the majority of us. This book is meant to be a resource for those difficult times, like when your child refuses to put on his shirt and you're already half an hour late for work, when your daughter is losing it over a low mark for the fourth time this month, or your son tells you "you're the worst parent ever." And if you've ever felt like you must be doing everything wrong or your child is headed towards disaster, we've been there with you. We may be clinicians, but we have both struggled in our parenting roles, and so we've only written about the stuff that's actually been helpful in our own personal lives. Not to say that you can't use the concepts in this book when things are going smoothly (in fact we hope you do!), but we also want to offer you something practical to try in those more challenging circumstances too. For those of you dealing with nonstop challenges, this book is also for you. We both work with families where one or more children and their parents are dealing with mental health concerns and major life stressors, and we find the approach outlined in this book to be helpful even when the problems have been around for a long time.

Obviously, there is no single, perfect manual for parenting. We are mental health professionals; you are the expert on your child. If some of our ideas strike you as useful, that's great. If others don't fit for you or your family, feel free to skip over to the next chapter. Parents these days can be faced with a constant sense that there is "one right way" to do things, and that simply isn't the case. It's also true that "timing is everything" and so we want to encourage you to sort out what might be best for your child in the way that feels most comfortable for you right now. You may even find that you feel differently about some of the content after you've been trying the skills for a while.

We also don't want to pretend that helping kids when they are most upset is a neat and tidy process. Life with family is messy at best, and sometimes it feels like total chaos. That's why we are ultra-motivated to share ideas and concrete strategies that we've found can actually help make a difference for you and your kids, whether they turn things around or even just take the edge off in the moment. We hope you'll customize them to fit your family's unique personality and your child's specific needs as a complement to the tools you already have. The framework is the roadmap, and your gut is your guide.

Finally, it is so important for you to know that you don't need to apply any of these ideas exactly for them to be effective. Not even close. The content of this book is grounded in the spirit of "effort counts twice" and "a little goes a long way." We've found that using any small bits from this book can amount to significant changes for your family over the course of days, weeks, and months together. Besides, there is no precision in parenting: We can only ever do our best to show up and be there for our kids, especially in the toughest of moments.

How to Use This Book

In our clinical practices, parents ask us every day, "But what do I say when … ?" or "Could you please write that down for me?" For parents of little kids, this may be ideas for getting through tantrums, like "I want a cookie!" while for parents of older kids, it can be staples like "I can't decide" or "I hate you." When we offered guidance to parents and care-givers, we used to tell them not to worry about the exact words they used and instead to embody a stance of validation when responding to these types of statements. In other words, it's not what you say, it's what you convey – and although that's true, parents would continue to ask for some scripts to help them to get started. In honor of these parents, we've organized the rest of the book into scenario-chapters, each starting with something your child may say, such as, "You love my sister more" or "I'm so stupid." The idea is that you can just flip to the section relevant to your family's life and get some ideas for now or later. We will provide a couple of possible response options for you to choose from, as well as tips for increasing the effectiveness of your efforts.

Each of these chapters will follow a similar pattern so that with repetition, it becomes more familiar to you, even second nature. For example, at the beginning of each scenario-chapter, we'll start by identifying the common *knee-jerk response* that many parents express when in that situation (ourselves included!). We'll then invite you to get curious about your child's perspective. We call this *building a bridge*, and it's a mental exercise that involves temporary entry into your child's world. Building a bridge may also require using what we refer to as an *emotion translator* to make sense of your child's experience. The emotion translator can come in handy when parents just don't understand what's going on with their children or there seems to be a disconnection between how they are behaving and what they really need (picture a kid screaming "You're not my real mom" but actually feeling vulnerable). Then it's time for *putting it into words* to *validate* their experience. This involves voicing a few reasons why it might make sense for your child to think their thoughts or feel their feelings. It helps to use kid-friendly language, or at least language friendly to your kid. The capacity to reflect someone else's internal experience, and without judgment, is a skill at the heart of all healthy relationships. It also happens to be the interpersonal process that has the most powerful effect on calming their brain in the moment, meaning it will also be *easier* to comfort them or even set limits once you've done so. Win–win. To help you with this step, we will present different options so that you can find the words that you think will work best in your situation. And by the way, you can communicate understanding of your child's point of view even if you don't agree with it in the slightest (picture a 5-year-old who is upset because the juice is red and not blue!). In other words, it's not *the* truth. It's their perspective, and this is an important distinction to carry with you. Which brings us to the final component of the model: *getting practical*. It's possible that the steps you've already taken are enough to prevent or calm the storm. If not, we'll propose solutions that you can choose from that are emotional and/or practical in nature and that help you and your child move forward together in a good way (and on to the next thing!). To demonstrate how to put it all together, we'll then include a *full script* of an interaction between an adult caregiver and a child, followed by *common pitfalls* that we've either experienced ourselves or encountered when supporting parents in our work. Finally, because this book is only one slice of the larger parenting pie, we've also included a list of resources and references that professionals and parents have found helpful to deepen the learning.

Here is a simple example of the approach "in action" to give you a sense of what we mean:

Remember the earlier scenario about the grocery store? Using the framework above, the *knee-jerk response* was reflected in the mom's initial reaction of: "C'mon; it'll be fun. You can choose the kind of cereal you want" and the dad's more hard-line approach: "You're coming to the store, and that's that."

Once we *build a bridge* into the child's world, however, we may discover that their son is easily bored at the grocery store, or he is embarrassed to be seen there with his parents and younger sibling. In other words, if we were to use an *emotional translator*, we'd hear something different from what was actually said, reflecting potentially vulnerable feelings that lie underneath, like "I'm worried my friends will make fun of me if they see me with you," for example.

To *put it in words*, you might then say:

> I can understand why you might not want to go to the grocery story. It's not the coolest place to hang out for a kid your age (Reason 1) and it might feel like an adult chore (Reason 2). I can also imagine there are a million things you'd rather do today (Reason 3).

Why do we suggest offering a few reasons as above? When the external environment (parents or other caring adults) reflects a child's inner thoughts and feelings *with sincerity* (sorry in advance to those who like to use sarcasm!), it activates a chain of brain-based events that decreases the intensity of their emotional experience – even if you don't agree with their experience and even if the bottom line is going to stay the same (going to the grocery store). In other words, when we as parents are able to voice what's going on inside of their head, the emotional orchestra in their brain actually quiets down. It's a neurobiological response that involves different chemicals and parts of the brain that basically work together to send a signal to the child that "Okay! I've been heard! I can cool my jets!" And so we have to admit upfront that we don't teach this style of responding just for the warm and fuzzies. Although that's often a bonus, our reasons are very practical too. We want to invite you to try this out because of the brain-calm it will create in your children, making them more likely to hear you, cooperate, and even come up with their own solutions to problems.

Enter the final step of our approach – *getting practical*. If you can relate to the preceding example, the truth is, you are going to the grocery store and that's not going to change. That being said, you can offer your child some compassion (emotional support) and a suggestion to help him pass the time (practical support): "I feel for you, bud. I really do. I can promise we won't be there all day. Why don't we figure out something for you to bring to help pass the time in the car, like your book or your music."

If you've already encountered the scenario described and it didn't go so well, there's always another chance to go back to your child and try again using the structure provided. We call this a "do-over," and it can be just as powerful as getting it right the first time. We actually can't emphasize this point enough. Whether your child is 9 or 49, it is never too late to try a new way of relating to them and with positive effects. Although this book is targeted to parents and caregivers of children, the principles can generalize across the life span with some tweaks.

All of this is what we refer to as "simple but not easy" because of those pesky knee-jerk responses that can make this new style of responding to our kids super uncomfortable. It's not uncommon for parents and caregivers to express reluctance when we provide them with strategies like the one we just outlined. Some worry about feeding the emotion or reinforcing it in an unhealthy way or giving their child too much power. These fears are normal, which is why we've dedicated Chapter 3 to addressing some of the most common concerns or potential "roadblocks." We've also devoted the whole of Chapter 4 to "staying on track" so that you don't forget to look after yourself when handling situations that might be triggering or just plain unpleasant.

The list of possible parenting scenarios is endless, so we encourage you to integrate the concepts for use in order to apply them when faced with a range of parenting challenges. We'll specifically address disagreements between partners in caregiving too. For example, how do you handle your child's other parent criticizing him or parenting in a way you don't like? Huge landmine. We've got you covered. After parents work with us using this method, whether individually or in groups, they often appreciate using the same skills with their partners, colleagues, and even their own parents. So, we hope these simple and effective strategies help you feel more confident getting through tough moments with your kids and beyond.

In the last few chapters, we offer recommendations for situations that require more intensive support as well as worksheets and handouts so you can take the ideas in the book a step further. While human emotions are universal, practical support strategies can vary according to the issue at hand, the age of the child, and other individual factors, so we aim to direct you towards references for some of our favorite resources.

By the way, throughout this book, we alternate between pronouns *she*, *he*, and *they*. We use the words *kid*, *child*, and *preteen* to refer to children of any gender. The words *parent* and *caregiver* are also used to describe any adult who is engaged in a caregiving relationship with a child. Likewise, we acknowledge that this adult may be of any gender and may be a biological or non-biological parent, family member, or other important adult in the child's life. Lastly, we know most parents don't have a lot of spare time, and so we'll say now that we are grateful that you've chosen to spend some of yours with us.

The Road Map   **2**

We invite you to let the following question anchor you during this next section: How many minutes would you be willing to invest to increase cooperation and collaboration with your child? What about to avoid a meltdown? What's reasonable to expect given your schedule and competing priorities? Twenty minutes? Ten minutes? Two minutes? Hopefully this is good news – the structure we are proposing can take as little as 90 seconds. That's right – less than 2 minutes. Now, it can take longer too – and sometimes a 5- or 10-minute investment yields the greatest reward, but we want you to know that we are proposing a brief approach to interaction that is most likely to calm the brain *enough* (not 100%) so that your child becomes more flexible in the moment and open to move on to the next thought, feeling, or activity.

Each of the chapters that make up the core of the book will follow the same general outline. Here we'll give you some additional background information on the steps we've outlined thus far so that, with practice, you will be able to apply them to your unique situations with flexibility. The framework includes first recognizing your knee-jerk response, then making a conscious choice to respond a little differently from what you may be used to, guided by these three components (in order): (1) building a bridge, (2) putting it into words, and (3) getting practical. These steps are considered in the context of a "calm-enough" parent-mind. In other words, you may not be totally calm, but you are calm enough to implement the steps with some degree of connection.

Recognizing the "Knee-Jerk" Response

Imagine your child comes home from school and says, "I suck at math. I will never get it." The almost universal response is to say something like: "No you don't," followed by something positive or uplifting or with a solution to the problem. We've surveyed literally thousands of parents, teachers, even clinicians, and these types of response are far and away the most common. Why? Because knee-jerk responses are usually borne out of our best intentions to care for our children: to protect them from harm and help them grow up to be happy, independent and productive adults. Unfortunately, we have been conditioned to believe that in order for this to happen, it is best to lean away from emotional discomfort and help others to do the same (more on that later). In addition to this powerful sociocultural influence, whether our children are in physical pain or emotional distress, most of us want it to go away as soon as possible, especially if their pain triggers within us feelings of helplessness (I have no idea how to help her!), anxiety (What if she disengages from school?), or other unpleasant emotional reactions (If she'd only study!). Regrettably, putting voice to those reactions doesn't help children move through the experience, and the last thing we want is for them to get stuck in the emotional quicksand. The more awareness you have of your knee-jerk responses, the better you will be able to pivot away from them to try something different. For example, in the face of your child's distress, are you more of a joker, a cheerleader, or a bright-side enthusiast? When it comes to your child's anger, do you get smaller or puff up? Take a moment to reflect on your go-to when one of your children is upset. Try to think of a specific child and a specific incident.

Categories of Knee-Jerk Responses

The following are categories of potential knee-jerk responses when in relationship with others. Can you recognize yourself in any one (or more) of these categories?

Reassuring	Downplaying	Problem-solving	Distracting
Telling them everything is going to be okay.	Helping them see the problem is not that big of a deal.	Giving them advice or suggestions about what they could do.	Changing the topic to something less stressful or painful.
Cheerleading	**I-dentifying**	**Questioning**	**Shoulding**
Helping them to focus on their positive qualities and potential.	Telling them about similar or worse things that have happened to you.	Trying to get more details so you can understand the situation.	Suggesting that they shouldn't feel a certain way.

Content adapted with permission from *The BC Children's Hospital Mind–Body Connection Group Treatment Manual* by A. Dhariwal, A. Chapman, T. Newlove, & E. Stanford. Unpublished treatment manual.

My knee-jerk response when my child is anxious is:

_____

_____

_____

My knee-jerk response when my child is sad is:

_____

_____

_____

My knee-jerk response when my child is embarrassed is:

_____

_____

_____

My knee-jerk response when my child is mad is:

_____

_____

_____

You may have noticed a different knee-jerk response depending on the feeling expressed by your child. This is because we've been socialized to respond to different emotions differently. You may have been taught to avoid anger in your own childhood home, or your avoidance of anger may have developed in reaction to having been exposed to too much anger as a child or teen. Either way, it can be helpful to be aware of your patterns of response to your child's expressions of vulnerability or her frustration and anger. That way, you can understand your patterns *and* have compassion for where these expressions come from. They do say that "the first 50 years of childhood are the hardest," and we're inclined to agree!

Step 1. Building a Bridge

Now it's time to build the bridge to lay the foundation for a new way of responding to situations that carry an emotional charge. What we need to remember, even during the worst times, is that we are not our children and they are not us. We are separate but connected. In moments of stress, you can think of you and your child like two islands: *Upset Child Island* and *Frustrated Parent Island*. When things start to go sideways and you're really lost, take the perspective of a curious explorer and ask yourself: *"I wonder what is going on with my child that she is acting this way?"* In other words, build a mental bridge to cross over to your child's experience, even if you are convinced she is being totally unreasonable. Whether you are correct in your assessment is irrelevant for this step – and thank goodness because a lot of what befuddles younger kids can be irrational, to put it mildly (think meltdown because of a missing sock). Finding a few different answers to this key question that make sense under the circumstances, and in light of your child's temperament, personality, and developmental stage, is key.

In other words, *building a bridge* lets parents get started by brainstorming a few educated guesses for why their child may be feeling or acting in a certain way. When first introduced to this step of the framework, some parents ask: "Why don't I just ask my kid why he is feeling this way?" If your child is in a headspace to have a conversation, that's great. You can ask him what's wrong and what he needs. That's the most straightforward approach and takes out any guesswork. But there are a number of scenarios in which the best option is to make a guess. These typically fall into one of four categories:

1. Children haven't yet learned to identify their feelings or needs.
2. They are too upset or overwhelmed to communicate clearly.
3. They feel uncomfortable with how they are feeling and therefore are not likely to be forthcoming.
4. They are upset with you and not in the mood to spill the beans.

In fact, we've found that educated guesses can be more valuable than it may seem on the surface because they also communicate to the child: "You are important to me and I am engaging in this mental exercise to try to get to know you in this moment. I am willing to get it wrong and try again."

The Emotion Translator

When you go to a new country and don't speak the language, you can sometimes make guesses about what's going on, but there will be times when you will need a translator to make sense of what people are saying. In an ideal world, kids would always be able to communicate what's wrong directly, in a nice enough way. In reality, and in particular in the situations described above, adults might need to mentally translate what kids say and do into something clearer or more logical until they become more capable of articulating their feelings and needs more directly. For example, sometimes children say things or act in ways that are inconsistent with what's really going on for them. A child who feels disconnected from you may tell you he hates you when really he is yearning for some attention and affection. When we see difficult behavior in our children, including harsh words or refusal to cooperate with reasonable expectations, most often, there is more to it. The renowned family therapist Virginia Satir described behavior as just the tip of the iceberg, with thoughts, feelings, and more below the surface where we can't easily see them (see Figure 2.1). When we can see what's underneath, even if we imagine it to be there, we can respond from a much calmer and connected place inside of ourselves.

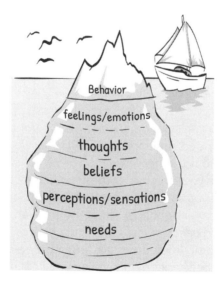

Figure 2.1 The personal iceberg

Adapted from: Satir, V., Banmen J., and Gomori, M. *The Satir Model Family Therapy and Beyond*. Palo Alto. CA: Science and Behavior Books Inc 1991.

Here's an example:
After being asked to stop texting with a friend, a tween shouts: "You ruin everything!"

Emotion translation. We could use the emotion translator to discover that what she is really trying to convey: "I'm *angry* at you because I don't want to stop chatting with one of my best friends."

Or another:
When Dad walks in the door after a business trip and strikes up a conversation with his partner, his son immediately runs to his room.

Emotion translation. The action might be communicating: "I'm really *angry* at you for being gone so long." Or maybe "I'm *sad* because I missed you and I want your attention too."

Translating outbursts and tantrums, negative behavior, and harsh words into emotions and needs can help us have the mind frame needed to then take our child's perspective.

When my child says/does: _____

I can imagine it's because she or he actually feels (vulnerable feeling):

_____

In these situations, it's possible she or he needs (vulnerable need):

_____

Don't worry if you can't quite generate ideas to understand the roots of emotionally charged statements or behaviors; we will provide many examples throughout the book to help you to get used to this way of thinking. We invite you to consider these possibilities or allow our suggestions to inspire you to figure out might be going on for your child. All you need to remember right now is that the emotion translator helps to translate *words* and *behavior* into *emotions* and *needs*. It means not taking kids literally sometimes, especially when they are really upset. This doesn't mean not believing them, but keeping in mind that all of us say and do all kinds of things when upset that may not reflect the more vulnerable parts of ourselves.

One more thing. Once you've successfully built a mental bridge, you don't need to stay over there indefinitely. The idea is to *temporarily* take the child's perspective so that you can help her move through her experience using the next steps (putting it into words and getting practical). It's a middle step in a longer process, and, remember, it has nothing, zero, nada, zilch, zip to do with the so-called truth.

Tips for Building a Bridge

One of the most efficient pathways for building a bridge to Child Island is by tuning in. In the busy life of parents, this is no small task. We don't mean you need to drop everything and focus on their mental state every minute of the day; that wouldn't even be in your child's best interest. But when children are upset and you have the resources to connect, focused attention – even for a few seconds – can be very helpful. To do so, we encourage you to do the following:

1. Move away from any distractions until the situation is resolved.
2. If other children are in the vicinity, let them know that you may not be able to attend to them for a few minutes.
3. Try to be silent for a few moments, take a few breaths and go inward.
4. Observe your child with curiosity and from that vantage point, see if you can feel what they may be feeling. It can also help to get down to their level.
5. If you can't get a sense for your child's experience, think about your child's day. Does he have a test coming up? Has she been complaining about problems with friends? Does he generally hate getting dressed in the morning? These are your clues.
6. Remember that they may sometimes talk like adults, but they don't think like adults. Four-year-olds think monsters are in their closet. Some 12-year-olds believe in the Tooth Fairy. Ask yourself why they might be reacting this way from their frame of mind, given their age, the circumstances, and your child's unique personality.
7. Think about how you may have felt as a kid if you were in your child's shoes.
8. If you still have no idea, just hang out with your child and let her know you're trying to understand her point of view and you want to help. Play or join in an activity with her for a while. Ask her for her input, or offer possibilities and see what happens.

Step 2. Putting It into Words

Once you've gone through the mental exercise of building the bridge, it is time to convey what you've learned on Child Island via the skill of validation or *putting it into words*. There exist many definitions in popular culture for what it means to validate someone. Some of them even contradict one another. For this reason, it's really important that we start off with a shared definition in the context of this particular framework. Whereas building the bridge is an internal exercise, our use of the term "validation" involves communicating to your child in words that you can imagine where they are coming from and why, regardless of whether you agree. We've found that these sentence starters can be really helpful to begin:

I could understand you …
I could imagine you …
No wonder you …
It would make sense that you …
When I put myself in your shoes I could imagine you …
… might feel/think/want to/not want to _____

You can use this structure to validate physical sensations ("I could imagine you might feel jittery inside!"), thoughts ("No wonder you think it's not fair"), or feelings ("It would make sense that you might feel sad"). Some kids might be more responsive to statements relating to any one of these categories, and so it can be worthwhile to give them all a try. That said, if you're pressed for time or can only remember one of the categories, research shows that the child's brain tends to respond best when feelings are labeled, and so we've provided you with a list of potentially helpful words in Chapter 23: Practical Resources.

Once you get started with one of these phrases, it's then time to offer a few possible reasons why your child might be feeling, thinking, or acting in the way they are. For example:

I could imagine you might be feeling upset because 1 (insert first possible reason here), because 2 (insert second possible reason here), and because 3 (insert third possible reason here).

Each of these statements has the power to help calm your child's brain to create flexibility for what's next (support, redirection, limits, etc.). With some kids, you will see the benefit with only one because-statement. Other kids need a bit more. For this reason, especially as you become more familiar with the approach, we recommend aiming for three because-statements. It will give you practice generating possibilities, and you'll be giving yourselves the best chance for success. That being said, don't worry if, in the moment, you can only come up with one or two. It's still going to be so different from a knee-jerk response that it's likely to have a positive effect.

Finally, when suggesting possibilities, it is important to reflect your belief in your child's "goodness." Children can sense what we think of them, whether we say it or not. If we interpret their behavior and experience in a way that suggests we think well of them and we know they want to do and be their best, this message will shine through. It doesn't mean false positivity, but a genuine recognition of their competence and underlying wish to please, to be understood, to feel accepted, to feel connected, to feel better), even if on the surface it doesn't always seem so. When parents can notice their child's good intentions and hold these in mind – through thick and thin – their child is more likely to follow a positive path moving forward. We not only support our child's growth through words and actions, but also through our belief in them.

Here is an example that highlights these ideas:
A child says: "This project looks terrible. I can't hand this in."
Their parent responds: "I can understand why you'd feel upset because (1) you really wanted the drawings to look more realistic and (2) you take your homework seriously. (3) You've also been working so hard, and you want your teacher to get that."

Notice a few things about this example: (a) the parent comments on the child's perspective rather than her own, (b) the parent shows she "gets it" by giving three possible reasons why the child might be feeling upset, and (c) the parent emphasizes the child's positive intention with each of the possibilities.

You might also have noticed that the parent doesn't rush in to fix or minimize the problem. This doesn't mean that reassurance and problem-solving don't have a role to play in this framework; on the contrary – they are crucial elements of the approach. It's just that the sequencing is what's most important. When parents lead with building a bridge and putting it into words, their efforts to comfort and support their child more practically will be met with increased openness and flexibility. How does it work? When you use the structure we are proposing, the verbal and nonverbal signals that come with validating the other's experience

Figure 2.2 Calming the brain

activates a release of brain-calming chemicals, including oxytocin, which then bind to receptors in their limbic system, otherwise known as the emotional center of the brain. It's like putting water on a fire. Once calm, they will be more flexible, more likely to engage in reason and problem-solving, and therefore more connected and cooperative.

Any chance you might feel a bit nervous about making educated guesses about the possible reasons why your child might be thinking or feeling a certain way? So normal. Some parents worry they will implant in their child's inner world an idea or a bad feeling that wasn't already there, while others worry about getting it wrong and losing their child's trust. They might then be drawn to engage in "Questioning" (one of the knee-jerk responses mentioned above) like in this scenario:

PARENT: "You look upset. What's wrong?"
CHILD: "Nothing."
PARENT: "Well, are you worried about something?"
CHILD: "I dunno."
PARENT: "Is it about school? Is it friends?"
CHILD: "I don't know!"
PARENT: "Honey, how can I help you if you don't tell me what the problem is?"

What to say instead? Not to worry. We will go over a multitude of examples so that you can support your child in a positive way without needing too many details about their specific problem. For now, we've found that as long as your because-statements are communicated in a tentative manner and with heart, they can be effective in some way. Offering educated guesses shows kids that parents have a handle on the situation and they are there to help kids understand and organize their thoughts and feelings. With this approach, parents convey that while they may not know the exact answer yet, they are confident they can lead the process of figuring it out with their child. They also communicate to the child in doing so that they can handle what might be going inside for them.

On the other hand, some kids may express annoyance if you suggest that you know exactly what they are thinking or feeling and why (especially if they are older and in a phase of trying to be more independent – you'll likely have a sense if this applies to you). This is a hazard for mental health professional parents like us who *love* to validate (ask our kids how annoying it can be, especially when we use our "therapist voice")! And so if that's your kid, it is important that your guesses are communicated in a way that is truly tentative, such as:

"I wonder if you might be feeling a little (insert emotion) or even (insert emotion) …"
"Maybe it's a little like …"
"I may be off here, but I could imagine that …"
"Some people would feel (insert emotion) in a situation like this …"
"I suppose that part of you might think/feel …"

 ## Step 3. Getting Practical

Despite all this attention on validation, we are certainly not suggesting that you spend three hours putting your child's thoughts and feelings into words. Validation helps kids make sense of their inner world and calm down, but they also need your help to move on, especially when they are younger (because of their immature brain) or the meltdown is intense (think five-alarm fire) or you're on the move (life keeps going). Enter the last part of our approach: *getting practical*. Underneath the anxiety, sadness, anger, and resistance lies a hidden need for something. Sometimes the need is emotional, like comfort, reassurance, or simply to feel heard. Sometimes the need can only be addressed through action, such that problem-solving or adult intervention may be required. Our "getting practical" component of the framework generally refers to short-term strategies, such as refocusing the child's awareness elsewhere, offering reassurance, supporting them with relaxation strategies, or solving a practical problem. There are many, many longer term, practical ways to help your child emotionally, such as doing mindful activities together, allowing lots of time for free play, and preparing them for tough moments in advance, but those go beyond the scope of this book. Please see our recommended reading section for more in-depth ideas depending on the situation with which you are faced.

Let's go back to our example from above to demonstrate the integration of this step.

CHILD: "This project looks terrible. I can't hand this in."

PARENT: "I can understand why you'd feel upset because you really wanted the drawings to look more realistic and you take your homework seriously. You've also been working so hard and you want your teacher to get that." (Putting it into words)

CHILD: "Yeah, I just don't know if I should spend time redoing the drawings or hand it in anyways?"

PARENT: "Sweetie, I believe in you, and I have a feeling that you'll make the right choice. Either way, I'm pretty sure it will work out." (Emotional support: communicating belief in the child)

This exchange might be enough to help the child sort it out on her own, or she may also need some practical help. For example, she might benefit from having the parent go through a list of pros and cons with her, help her to remember more realistic ways of thinking, or set a bedtime limit like this:

CHILD: "This project looks terrible. I can't hand this in."

PARENT: "I can understand why you'd feel upset because you really wanted the drawings to look more realistic, and you take your homework seriously. You've also been working so hard, and you want your teacher to get that." (Putting it into words)

CHILD: "Yeah, I just don't know if I should spend time redoing the drawings or hand it in anyways?")

PARENT: "Sweetie, I believe in you, and I have a feeling that you'll make the right choice. Either way, I'm pretty sure it will work out." (Emotional support: communicating belief in the child)

CHILD: "No, Mom! I don't know what to do!"

PARENT: "How about this: I will give you half an hour to redo some of the drawings. After half an hour, it's time to stop. I will let you know when you have 10 minutes left." (Practical support: providing structure and setting a limit)

CHILD: "Okay – but give me 5 minutes to get myself ready before starting the timer!"

Here are other examples of ways you can offer emotional and practical support to your child:

Emotional Support Ideas

- Offer comfort in words or with physical affection ("Come here and I'll give you a hug")
- Provide reassurance ("I believe it will be OK")
- Communicate acceptance and non-judgment ("It's totally normal to feel that way")
- Communicate togetherness and availability ("We're in this together," "I'm here for you")
- Communicate trust or belief in the child, his abilities, his good intentions ("I believe you can get through this")
- Share enjoyment with your child ("Wow – that is so cool!")
- Allow space (space can be physical or psychological *and* time-limited; the plan for reconnection must be clearly communicated ("Why don't I give you some space and I'll check back in with you in 5 minutes").

Practical Support Ideas

- Redirect your child to another thought or activity (e.g., playing a game, engaging in a physical activity, listening to music)
- Teach and practice communication and social skills (e.g. teaching assertiveness)
- Teach and practice mindfulness, self-compassion, and relaxation skills (e.g. noticing the red objects in the room; reminding the child that everyone struggles sometimes; belly breathing)
- Support your child to face fears (e.g. doing difficult things with exposures to the anxiety-provoking thing or situation in a gradual, step-by-step way)

- Use positive reinforcement (e.g. praising and/or rewarding desirable behaviors)
- Help your child to brainstorm ideas for a solution (e.g. taking turns coming up with possible ideas)
- Offer solutions to help solve the practical problem or take over to solve the problem (e.g. suggesting that this is a problem that needs adult help)
- Offer a few choices or some degree of control over the situation (e.g. narrowing the options for the child)
- Set a limit (e.g. being clear about expectations or what needs to happen)
- Just be with your child and let the feelings run their course.

Okay, let's summarize what we've covered so far. When you put into words your child's thoughts or feelings as if you were a mirror to his inside voice, reflecting a few possibilities that connect with his goodness, it helps the child's brain get unstuck, or at least become more flexible. Once in this more open state, it's time to offer emotional and practical support. It is so, so important to reiterate that the sequencing of the steps is critical because the two steps complement one another in the order we've described. It also bears repeating that although it's not a perfect solution, this framework typically works much faster than if you were to jump immediately to providing emotional or practical support such as reassurance, offering an alternative perspective or limit-setting. Check out these scenarios (Figures 2.3 and 2.4) to see if you can feel the difference.

Getting Ready to Put It Together

Are the dialogues making you cringe because they don't sound realistic? Hopefully that doesn't stop you from reading on. We'll provide the ideas, but we implore you to edit the language and delivery to make it work better for you and your child. We'll also give you lots of workspace in the book to figure out your own version. And we acknowledge that, to some degree, the responses aren't fully realistic since they're a just a snapshot of what is possible. However, we wish we could share with you the many anecdotes from parents who were very skeptical at first but who made a commitment to following the steps and were pleasantly surprised with

Figure 2.3 The knee-jerk response

what transpired. There is no quick fix in human relationships, and the structure described in this book won't work 100% of the time. But it is more likely to improve both your relationship with your child and your own well-being as a parent.

Feeling overwhelmed? Forget everything we shared so far. For now, just remember that building a bridge to speak your child's inner thoughts and emotions has a similar effect to the breath in calming the brain and body. A child – regardless of their age – who receives validation is able to think more clearly, solve problems more effectively, and engage with others more collaboratively. Some children may need the equivalent of one or two deep "breaths of validation" before they can accept your emotional or practical support, whereas others might need a bit more, but the process itself is pretty universal.

Figure 2.4 Validation and support

Potential Roadblocks   **3**

You may feel like this approach makes sense and you're willing to jump ahead to get started. Or, maybe you read our suggestions in Chapters 1 and 2 and thought "Sure, it sounds nice on the page, but you haven't met *my* kid" or "That doesn't sound like something I'd ever say" or "I'm not sure this is a good idea." Whatever you're thinking at this moment, we hope you'll read on as we try to address some of the more common reactions that may arise as you engage with this book and try out these new strategies. We'll handle some of the most common ones up front in this chapter and weave others into each scenario-chapter under the *Pitfalls* section.

Some of the most common concerns parents voice about using this framework include the following:

1. Won't focusing on negative emotions and behaviors just reinforce them?
2. When there's a problem or my child is upset, shouldn't I be focused on finding a solution?
3. Our life is too busy. I just don't have time for this level of engagement with my children every time they are upset.

These are totally legitimate concerns. Keeping these in mind, the *knee-jerk response* makes a lot of sense because the goal is usually to help by interrupting the child's challenging emotion or behavior as quickly as possible. At first glance, it addresses all three of the main concerns just listed. So before we ask you to try something a little different, let's explore some of the logic behind our more automatic responses.

When Children Have Big Feelings

Nothing quite prepares you for the intensity of feelings that comes when you become a parent or caregiver. Every instinct tells you to protect the child from harm, and you would do anything to keep them safe. You probably remember the first time your child was hurt or sick, even if it was just a cold. All we want is for them to feel better as quickly as possible. It's no different when our child is in emotional pain. Try this: Your child comes home from school and cries out: "I'm a loser and nobody likes me." What is your automatic response? Chances are it will sound like this: "No you're not – you're great!" or "Why would you feel that way?" or "Forget them – they're just jealous!" All of these responses are normal. As parents, almost nothing is more stressful than when our child is really upset. It's even worse when we don't know what to do to solve their problem. All we want to do is make it stop.

Let's take another example, but this time instead of being sad or worried, our child is angry or oppositional. If a child you care about says: "I hate you! You don't know anything!" what is your first reaction? For most of us, it might be a version of "Don't speak to me that way!" or "Get up to your room!" Again, completely natural. This time, our first concern isn't helping our child feel less pain, but it's still "making it stop." We don't want disrespect or anger to go on or get out of hand. We want to nip the problem in the bud so that our child develops into a respectful member of society.

The issue is that the most recent advances in neuroscience are suggesting that these old methods don't work so well. Trying to stop the storm is not as effective as hanging in there with our children and supporting them to get through it. In fact, it can be counterproductive to interrupt emotional processes too frequently in that kids then don't develop *emotional self-efficacy*, which is a term that refers to confidence and skill in managing stress and distress and has been linked to all kinds of positive outcomes later in life. In other words, we don't want to help our kids to feel better; we want to help our kids to get *better at feeling* – as in to feel their feelings with confidence and skill so that they eventually develop healthy coping skills (and avoid the adoption of unhealthy strategies to avoid feeling bad). So then why can we be so focused on wanting to make it stop?

We Are Brain-Wired to Our Children

When our children suffer, so do we. In fact, there is an old saying: "As a parent, you are only as happy as your least happy child." Neuroscience is revealing the truth of that statement. Consider this: When one of my children cuts a finger, I immediately shudder. It's an immediate instinct, before any time for rational thought or even worry. How does that happen? It turns out that humans are wired for empathy: the ability to understand and share the feelings of another. There are some interesting studies that illustrate the point. Neuroscientist Tania Singer and her colleagues used brain scans (functional MRI) to study what happens when you watch a loved one experience pain. Her study showed that just witnessing the pain of a loved one lights up the areas of your *own* brain involved in those very same feelings. It's like an internal mirror reflecting the other person's pain. In fact, you may have heard about the *mirror neuron system*. Mirror neurons are brain cells that fire when a person observes someone else's action or experience. They help explain why even young babies cry when they see another baby cry or why we smile automatically when someone smiles at us. In other words, these neurons "mirror" the feeling of another person, as though the observer were itself the one feeling. The intensity of the mirror neuron response seems to parallel the intensity of the emotional bond with the other person. Imagine you hear that an acquaintance from work got injured. Now imagine it's your next-door neighbor. What if it's your sister or partner? Or the worst of all – your child. It's almost cruel of us to even suggest that, but we do so to illustrate the point that our children draw a much stronger physical and emotional reaction than anyone else. It may be because we love them so much or see them as vulnerable, and it may also be because having children actually wires our brains for caring, and especially for our offspring. No wonder we try to show our children the bright side or use distraction to move them to a new thought, feeling or activity! When they feel pain, so do we. When they feel happy again, we feel relief – for their sake and for ours.

Lucy's 6-year-old son Oliver has always been a little on the shy side. He did pretty well with the transition to kindergarten. But halfway through the year, the teacher went on leave, and Oliver started having major tantrums each morning. Rationally, Lucy knew full well that the new teacher was great and that Oliver could cope just fine, but every morning, when

Oliver started to scream and cry, she could feel her heart start to beat faster and her muscles tensed. After a while, she started bracing herself for Oliver's reaction.

Why was Lucy's body reacting so intensely to her son's distress?

The short answer is that this is nature's alarm system. Our ancestors needed to be able to protect and care for their young in a variety of situations. Babies and young children would not be able to survive alone in the wild, so their parents had to be wired to protect them. Babies and young children also lack the verbal skills to communicate what's wrong – their body language, cries, and facial expressions have to do the trick. So of course we respond when our children send off even the smallest distress signals! Parents are nature's megaphone for children's cries.

We Want to Be "Good" Parents

Jenna works part time as a social worker in a downtown neighborhood. She's also a foster mother to two children. She considers herself to be a compassionate and competent person and strives to be an emotion-friendly parent. For her foster daughter Chloe's third birthday, Jenna decides to take her to the toy store to pick out her own birthday gift. As they walk down the aisles, Jenna delights in Chloe's smile and enthusiasm. When they get to the row of stuffed animals, Chloe's eyes widen, and she grabs three animals off the shelf, clutching them all tightly, and says, "I want these!" Jenna looks at Chloe's little face and the stuffed giraffe, pig, and dog she's holding. What a dilemma. Does she say yes to all three, making Chloe happy, even though she only intended to buy one gift? Or does she say no, risking a tantrum on what's supposed to be her special day? This poor little girl has already been through so much in her young life. As Jenna takes a moment to think, an older woman walks down the same aisle. She decides that she should stick to her principles and tries to avoid using the word "no" by saying: "Pick the one you love most and the other two can stay here and play with their friends." Not to be fooled, Chloe starts screaming, "No! I want all of them!" Now Jenna is acutely aware of the older woman's seemingly disapproving stare. It gets to her, and she starts to feel embarrassed. Now she feels more pressure as she decides what to do next.

Nobody sets out to do a bad job as a parent. We all want to do our best. Despite this, we all struggle with insecurities, and we want to avoid embarrassment. We are also members of a society where parent shaming and blaming goes on in all spheres of life, from social media to workplaces to mommy groups and, unfortunately, in our own families. There may even be an unwritten assumption that parents are to blame for the negative things their children experience, including their displays of "negative" emotion. To top it off, our own inner critic may be loud enough for all to hear. For these reasons, we as parents can be motivated to shut down our children's sadness or anger, and especially in public or in front of family or friends. As mental health professionals, we can certainly relate to this vignette. When going out to the mall or for dinner, our worst nightmare is running into clients and colleagues when things are upside down or sideways with our own family! We're supposed to be the pros after all! We can assure you – we are just as human as you are, especially behind closed doors.

We Don't Want Our Kids to Become Soft or Entitled

A common concern we hear about responding to our kids' feelings is that we do them no favors by making them "soft" when the world around us is "hard." After all, our kids' coaches, professors, and bosses aren't going to validate their feelings. This isn't how the real world operates. And if we talk about feelings when they have just done something wrong, there is a concern that then they are basically getting away with the bad behavior. They need to learn right from wrong and how to behave properly in society. Sound familiar?

We agree fully that we need to set our sights on supporting our children to develop resilience to manage the adversity they will surely come across. We also agree that kids need to be taught right from wrong. We have just learnt from research (and experience!) that the educational messages don't go in very well when kids are super upset. Usually, when we give a punishment without addressing the underlying emotions, kids then learn to behave to avoid punishment, without having internalized the motivation to do differently next time because it's right or good. They also end up feeling at odds with adults. Colleague Dr. Dan Siegel contends (and we agree) that connection is what opens a child's ears to redirection, guidance, and the will to do good above all else. In other words, when we can connect on an emotional level, it actually helps consequences have more meaning for kids.

As to getting along in the real world, decades of research has shown that kids who are raised with more discussion about their emotions learn to regulate their upset feelings more easily and function better in a number of areas, including academic performance, social skills and physical health. These kids and teens also experience fewer "negative" emotions overall, have greater self-worth, and develop the ability to become more independent. It's kind of like armor against inner and outer adversity. When we can accurately reflect kids' thoughts and feelings and help them to sort them out, they relate better to others too. Another win–win.

We Don't Want to Make Them More Upset

There is a widely held perception in popular culture that leaning into an emotion can create a landslide. That somehow if we acknowledge our child's pain, it will intensify it to the point of overflow. And to be honest, there is a grain of truth to this. If a child's lip is quivering and his eyes are beginning to water, and you attend to his sadness, it is likely that the tears will start to flow. Emotions rise, and they pass. That is their nature. But thankfully it just isn't true that our children will become stuck in a never-ending cycle of feeling when we validate them or support them to express their need – even if that need is simply to feel heard. In fact, we are more likely to feel stuck in our feelings when we try to push them away. When it comes to distress, famed psychologist Carl Jung's perspective was, "what you resist not only persists, but will grow in size."

Just for fun (and we fully acknowledge that we have a nerdy definition of what it means to have fun ☺), imagine you just lost your job, and when you tell your best friend how upset you are, she immediately replies, "Oh, you'll be fine. Want to go get a latte?" Even though it's a silly example, we know this would still feel bad. That's what it can feel like to kids when they're really upset and we try to minimize their problem or we are quick to reassure them or change the subject. If instead we can talk about some of the painful feelings our child is experiencing, they will feel more heard and understood, and this will help them to ride the emotional wave.

> Listen earnestly to anything [your children] want to tell you, no matter what. If you don't listen eagerly to the little stuff when they are little, they won't tell you the big stuff when they are big, because to them all of it has always been big stuff.
>
> (Catherine M. Wallace)

Their Pain Hits Close to Home (Too Close Sometimes)

If as a child, it was difficult for you to make friends, it may be especially hard for you to respond in an emotionally attuned way in the event your child encounters social challenges. In other words, when our child's pain reminds us of our own pain, we hurt twice: once for them in the present and once for ourselves in the past. If it's a particularly big hurt, we may not recognize the influence it still has on us because our memory has a sneaky way of protecting us from painful feelings too. So it's a bit of a leap of faith to ask yourself: if a situation with your child repeatedly feels really overwhelming or ends in disaster, could it be that it's opening up a box in your brain that comes from the past? These hot spots are usually to do with our own parents and families or the things that happened to us when we were young. It certainly helps to become aware of the particular triggers we have, and this awareness can help you with some of the strategies we'll discuss in the chapters ahead.

We Don't Have Time

We are busy. We have other responsibilities. We have places to get to. It's unfortunate timing that many meltdowns occur right before or during transitions. The more rushed we feel, the worse it seems to go. How often do we say to ourselves; "I don't have time for this!" In these situations, we are usually less likely to feel helplessness and worry and more impatience and frustration. Especially when the reason behind the outburst is seemingly irrational. I'm talking about when your 4-year-old can't get dressed because his "underwear isn't comfortable" or your 12-year-old isn't doing homework because her "teacher is a jerk." The more rushed we feel, the more we can kick into high gear and repeat the same instruction over and over to get kids moving: "Okay kids, time to get dressed please … Kids! It's time to get dressed … Hey! I said it's time to get dressed … CLOTHES – NOW!"

MY KIDS 30 MINUTES BEFORE IT'S TIME TO GO

MY KIDS 2 MINUTES BEFORE IT'S TIME TO GO

You'd think that with how often we engage the strategy of repetition, it would be a sure thing. Unfortunately – and you don't need us to tell you this – it doesn't usually speed things up, at least not without escalating to threats of consequences, which can then further escalate the situation when your kid is feeling really stuck in an emotional storm. And so it can actually end up taking a lot *more* time not to address what might be going on underneath. If you often find yourself in a rut with your child when there's a time pressure, it may be worth experimenting to see if this approach may actually save you time or at least decrease the tension in the home while getting the job done. Remember: How much time are you prepared to invest to avoid a meltdown or increase engagement? Hopefully we can convince you to give it a shot for a couple of minutes – for their sake but also for yours!

We Were Conditioned to Do So

Remember when your child was a toddler and you would do literally anything – including dance like a fool – if it meant she would stop crying? This is actually a cultural phenomenon. Simple as that. When our child is in distress – in other words – when they feel sad, mad or afraid, we often make desperate attempts to transform their pain with distraction or other techniques. We will even go so far as to try to convince our children that they shouldn't be feeling the way they do: "There's no need to be upset – it's not a big deal"; "You're just [hungry or tired]." Why? Because this is what we were taught to do, and for generations.

We've also been conditioned to be "fixers." If a child cuts himself badly enough to need stitches, we don't hesitate to get him patched up. There is a clear-cut action that fixes the problem. Similarly, with emotional wounds and upsets, we have been socialized to take action (don't just stand there, do something!), with less time spent learning how to comfort others emotionally. It can feel like just listening or talking aren't *really* doing anything or not doing enough, and it can make parents feel ineffective, useless, or helpless to *just sit there*. Yet children really value our attentive presence. Often, they appreciate our presence and willingness to listen open-mindedly even more than any practical suggestions about how to solve the problem. Have you ever watched the YouTube video "It's Not About the Nail"? Highly recommended if you feel like your loved one just doesn't appreciate your advice, no matter how good it is!

To complicate matters further, even though all emotions have biological functions, we've come to categorize them as "bad" and "good," and so emotional pain and happiness can feel like opposites for many. Our society's "pursuit of happiness" can also put a lot of pressure on parents to "raise happy kids." If the definition of happiness is the absence of suffering, then of course we want to make our kids' upset feelings go away as quickly as possible. Take for example when you bring your child to the dentist for the first time. The first instinct can be to reassure him beforehand, "Don't worry, it will be okay." Or maybe to reassure him during the procedure: "It's almost done!" At the heart of our efforts is a deep wish for him *not* to worry and *not* to hurt. The same is true of emotional pain. If your daughter comes home from school and says no one played with her at recess or her friends insulted her on social media, you'd give anything to take that hurt away. You don't want her to be sad; you want her to be happy, and the most common strategy we've been taught to move from sad to happy is to reassure, distract and problem-solve.

Take a moment, close your eyes and imagine a time when you felt rejected as a child or teen. Remember who was there, what was said, and how it felt. Now imagine you finally connect with a trusted caregiver, and you tell her how badly it felt to experience the exclusion. She responds with: "I'm sure they didn't mean it" or "Anyone would be lucky to hang out with you." Feel better? If so, chances are it will only be temporary. Reassurance can bring short-term relief, there's no doubt. But if it's the only strategy, children can be left feeling alone in their pain or with the impression that the adult can't handle "going there" with them. There is only one thing worse than being excluded at school, and that's having nobody to talk to about how bad it can feel.

To bring awareness to the ways in which your early experiences shaped your response patterns, consider the following questions:

Which displays of emotion were most taboo in my home growing up?

Anxiety   Sadness   Embarrassment   Anger   Other: _____

How did I work through my feelings of anxiety? What kind of support did I get from the adults in my life?

_____

_____

_____

How did I work through my feelings of sadness? What kind of support did I get from the adults in my life?

_____

_____

_____

How did I work through my feelings of embarrassment? What kind of support did I get from the adults in my life?

_____

_____

_____

How did I work through my feelings of anger? What kind of support did I get from the adults in my life?

_____

_____

_____

How did these experiences affect my comfort with supporting my child's expression of:

Anxiety:

_____

_____

_____

Sadness:

_____

_____

_____

Embarrassment:

_____

_____

_____

Anger:

_____

_____

_____

Other:

_____

_____

_____

Counter-Conditioning: Going against the Grain to Weather the Storm Together

In the best of times, your child will respond to your new manner of communication with love and gratitude. You will literally see the effects of the calming neurochemicals right before your eyes, and in seconds. When they are overwhelmed and almost overboard, however, you may feel like you're dealing with a hurricane. They may literally whirl around or cry and scream and be totally out of control. We often expect more from older kids because they may seem more physically organized, but actually they can lose control of their emotions too. They may swear, dig in their heels, and refuse to do things or generally act in ways that are unpleasant. It's during these times that kids really need their parents to help them weather the emotional storm. One preteen described feeling like she was drowning in "emotion soup." She knew something big was going on, but she had no idea how to make sense of it, much less what to do to make it stop. That's because the brain structures responsible for regulation aren't fully developed until adulthood, and even then, the capacity to manage one's emotions comes from co-regulation and practice, and some kids need more of it than others.

This means that as much as we may all want to avoid pain and disruption, the only way out of emotion is actually through it. Sigh – it's true. If we sidestep emotion, over time it may build up or come out in other ways, usually with unhealthy behaviors like aggression, zoning out with the Internet or food, or, in some situations, it can increase the possibility of serious mental health symptoms like substance use and self-harm. If, instead, we can work with our emotions (even the unpleasant ones), we find that they eventually pass and we gain the confidence that we can manage them in the future. This process of working through feelings is what we want to suggest you learn to do with your children using the easy-to-use framework we are proposing. And by easy-to-use, we mean easy-to-use-most-of-the-time and practice, practice, practice. And when it's not-at-all-easy-to-use-are-you-shrinks-for-real?, Chapter 4 can be a really helpful resource. So now that we are committed to interrupting these societal and intergenerational patterns of emotion avoidance (right?), it's good to ready our mindset. How you ask? Maya Angelou says it best:

> Hoping for the best, prepared for the worst, and unsurprised by anything in between.
>
> (Maya Angelou)

Staying on Track $\qquad$ 4

We are not exaggerating when we say that caring for a child is probably the hardest job any of us will ever do. It is probably the most rewarding too, but if you're like most parents and caregivers, that doesn't really matter in the middle of a total crisis. And when we are stressed, overtired, or just plain irritable, we can lose control and say or do things we later regret. The good news is that we can increase our capacity to choose what we say and what we do by checking in with ourselves and engaging our nervous system to our advantage. After this chapter, we'll (finally!) be getting on with the meat of this book and providing you with ways to respond to challenging parenting scenarios. In order to do this, it is important to be calm enough ourselves. Not necessarily peaceful and Zen, but reasonably calm. If your head is about to explode in frustration, trying to squeeze yourself into some recommended words probably won't have the desired effect.

By the way, as clinicians, parents, and fellow humans, we have zero expectation that you will always remain level-headed. It's actually strange for kids when they do something really aggravating and a parent responds with forced calm. In other words, it's normal to react! The key is that, while making sure the reaction is genuine, it's best if it doesn't escalate your child further or hurt your relationship. Again, nothing needs to be (or can be) perfect. You can almost always address a reaction that's gone awry, but we want to set you up for a higher chance of success. So how does one keep some balance in the face of total kid meltdowns? This chapter reviews new and well-known strategies that can be used to refocus or reorient when we're on the edge ourselves. We'll also highlight some of the ideas we've found most helpful personally, with clients and from research on parenting stress.

The Breath Is the Brain's Remote Control

Although highly underrated, the simple act of taking a few deep breaths does help to get the space needed to figure things out in the middle of a chaotic situation. How? Scientists have found that the breath is like the remote control for our nervous system. If you take a series of quick shallow breaths, your sympathetic nervous system will activate as if in the face of danger. Likewise, inhaling slowly and deeply through the nose activates the parasympathetic nervous system, which is responsible for bringing our body back to baseline. When our nervous system calms, so too does our mind, allowing us to regain access to the capacities for reason and logic that were previously blocked by stress. That's why when we are highly emotional we are more likely to do or say something we regret once we regain our composure. We've all "lost it" with our kids at one time or another, and those memories can feel pretty bad – we have quite a few that are cringe-worthy ourselves (and isn't it amazing just how incredible children's memories can be for our bloopers?). Thankfully, a couple of deep inhales can cut that risk dramatically. It's also a technique that is there for you anytime, anyplace, and in front of anyone, and it comes with zero side effects.

Simple Breathing Exercises in the Moment

1. Belly Breathing

    a. Place one hand on your chest and the other on your belly. This will allow you to feel your diaphragm move as you breathe.
    b. Breathe in slowly through your nose so that your stomach moves out against your hand.
    c. Exhale slowly through your mouth, keeping your lips open, but close together so that you can hear the breath escape.
    d. Repeat until you feel calmer.

2. Counting while Breathing

    a. Inhale for a count of three.
    b. Hold for a count of three.
    c. Exhale for a count of three.
    d. Repeat until you feel calmer.

You can use these techniques before engaging with your child or in the heat of the moment. Yes it may seem silly, odd, or impractical to take a breathing break in the middle of a heated debate or while your child is having a tantrum in front of you. However, doing so will greatly reduce your potential for reactivity, and you will benefit from the power of mirror neurons in that your child may also calm down some by watching you regain composure.

Self-Compassion in the Midst of Crisis

If possible, after or while breathing, notice that your child is upset and that you are upset too. Remind yourself that it's normal to be upset in this situation and that many other parents would feel exactly the same way. Tell yourself that on some level, it makes sense for your child as well. If it feels like the right thing to do, you can acknowledge that your internal "parent alarm" is going off. You may even recognize one of the common triggers that set it off, like the ones we referenced in Chapter 3. Chances are, you may not immediately have time or space to recognize the sensations, emotions, or thoughts that come along with your internal alarm, and that's okay. That may be something to reflect on after the storm has passed. During the moment, you may, however, want to pause just to acknowledge that you and your child are in a tough spot and that you're doing the best you can. Engaging in this way can help us to find our footing again.

Dr. Kristin Neff is the mother of a child with autism and also one of the leading experts in the field of self-compassion. She developed a brief exercise called the Self-Compassion Break. We have found this works well for parents and caregivers in the midst of difficult times with their children.

Dr. Kristin Neff's Self-Compassion Break

To begin, say to yourself:

1. **This is a Moment of Suffering**
    That's mindfulness. Other options include:

    This hurts.
    Ouch.
    This is stress.

2.   **Suffering is a Part of Life**
     That's common humanity. Other options include:

     Other people feel this way.
     I'm not alone.
     We all struggle in our lives.

Now, put your hands over your heart, feel the warmth of your hands and the gentle touch of your hands on your chest. Or adopt the soothing touch you discovered felt right for you.

Say to yourself:

3.   **May I be Kind to Myself**
     You can also ask yourself, "What do I need to hear right now to express kindness to myself?" Is there a phrase that speaks to you in your particular situation, such as:

     May I give myself the compassion that I need.
     May I learn to accept myself as I am.
     May I forgive myself.
     May I be strong.
     May I be patient.

This practice can be used any time of day or night and will help you remember to evoke the three aspects of self-compassion when you need it most.

Source: www.selfcompassion.org; reprinted with permission

Briefly Focus on Something Besides the Problem

Remembering to breathe or to be kind to oneself doesn't work for everyone all the time. For some people, it helps to pay attention to things outside of oneself to refocus with a new set of eyes and a calmer mind and body. Using any of your six senses – vision, hearing, taste, smell, touch, or the perception of your body – can also help to trigger a reset.

Sensory Reset

1.   Look around at objects in the room. Notice their color or shape. Carefully examine a picture or plant.
2.   Take out your headphones and listen to a soothing piece of music.

3. Eat a fruit slowly, taking time to notice the aroma, texture, and taste.
4. Take out some of your favorite essential oils. A simple smell can do the trick.
5. Hold a pillow and notice how it feels. Feel the fabric under your skin.
6. Stretch your arms overhead or do circles with your wrist, noticing the movement.
7. Give your arm a gentle squeeze or wrap yourself in a hug.

You can even focus your senses on your child in this way to help you to feel calmer in the moment (although we don't recommend you start to smell them!). Take a few seconds to look at your child as if you were seeing her for the first time. Notice her appearance, the tone of her voice. Try to pay attention to what she is saying, listening carefully to her choice of words. Doing so will help you to feel calmer, even in the midst of challenging interactions. It also helps to see new possibilities for solutions for when you are ready to reengage.

Let Your Child Know a Bit About How You're Feeling

While some parents react more strongly than they'd like to, other parents may hold too much back. If you're a parent who always tries to be strong for your child and keeps your own feelings mostly hidden so as not to burden him, it can sometimes help to share a little bit more. We definitely don't recommend doing so with the expectation the child will comfort you or to relay how upset you are so the child will feel badly, yet censoring your own feelings completely can leave your child feeling confused (because they sense something is going on anyway) and cause the pressure to build up inside you even more. Saying something simple and genuine like: "I'm struggling right now with how to be here for you" or "I'm worried about how we're talking to each other" can help both you and your child feel calmer.

Take an Actual Break

Although we really encourage caregivers to stay with children as much as possible while they are upset, sometimes parents need some space to settle and to come back to themselves. Ideally, you have already communicated to your children that sometimes parents need to take breaks to calm down. That way, when it happens, there is some point of reference for your child that can help them cope while you're "away." If you use this strategy, you must also let your child know that you will be back to reconnect with her in a few minutes so that she doesn't feel rejected or left alone in her distress. She may still react to your need for a break with increased upset, especially if she is younger, and so it is important to be aware that this reaction is normal and to reengage as soon as possible. If your child is of preschool age, you can say, "Mommy/Daddy needs a break to calm down so I can help you. I will be right here – I am not leaving." If you need to go into another room, do not lock children outside, as this can lead to them feeling panicked about the separation. If your child is of school age, you can say, "I need a break right now. I'm still with you, I just need some quiet to think and breathe so I can help you in the best way possible. We can talk again in 5 minutes." Depending on their personality, it could even be helpful to set a timer to help them to handle the stress of waiting. Finally, it is important to remember that in these situations, the break is for the parent. It's not necessarily what the child wants or needs, and so it is a go-to strategy when it's just not possible to calm down in your child's presence and you are out of options.

How to Know When You Need a Minute (or More)

1. You are debating back and forth with your child, and it isn't going anywhere.
2. You feel yourself getting more and more frustrated (rising voice, tensing muscles, feeling hot) or you feel overwhelmed, helpless, or hopeless.
3. Your child looks to you like they are purposely trying to hurt or manipulate you.
4. You feel the urge to hurt your child verbally or physically.
5. You start arguing with your co-parent or other adults about the child's emotions or behaviors in the midst of the child's meltdown.
6. You start blaming yourself or others for your child's upset or negative behaviors.

It's Not Personal and the Power of the Mantra

When overwhelmed with emotion, kids (and adults) are more likely to blame others for their pain than to reflect on their inner states. Most kids generally haven't learned to recognize that just because they're upset doesn't mean it's someone else's fault. That means that in these moments, if your child screams "I wish you weren't my dad!" it's not 100% related to what you did or didn't do. Let's couple this with fascinating research that shows that when we are stressed, we are more likely to take things personally because our neurological default mode in this state is to protect and defend. This means that in the scenario just described, you may feel the urge rise within you to respond with some sort of defense or counterattack. So far, we've explained how parents are brain-wired to their kids. The connection is true in reverse. Kids know they are most safe and secure with the people who love them most, so they are more likely to let loose and blame them most harshly. When your kid is stressed, and so are you, it can be helpful to harness the power of the mantra. Mantras have been used for centuries and can change mind-tracks, especially when the record in our brain is skipping (do people still use records?!). When we are triggered and we can't calm our own brain-storm fast enough, mantras can take the edge off just enough to stay above water. The spiritual teacher Eckhart Tolle shares: "It is never the situation that cause suffering, it is our thoughts about it." A mantra such as "It's not about me, it's not about me" or "We love each other even when we fight, we love each other even when we fight," or "She's just a kid, she's just a kid" can help you to calm yourself enough to show up in a way that is more likely to be loving and productive.

Phone a Friend

It's not just a lifeline on a popular game show! Nothing compares to the relief that comes from telling a good friend how badly things have gone, knowing they won't judge us or that they've been through the same or worse with their own kids. During the heat of an argument or meltdown, there often isn't much time, but taking a few minutes to text or call a co-parent or helpful friend or family member may be worth it if it supports a system reset.

Marvel at the Absurdity of Life with Kids

And finally … Some people do really respond well to a comedy break, even in the darkest times. When things are at their worst, you may need some help to dig your sense of humor out from under the heaps of gar-bage you're living through in this moment. There's a reason why the parody book *Go the F**k to Sleep* by Adam Mansbach became a *New York Times* bestseller and shelves are lined with tongue-in-cheek books like *I Just Want to Pee Alone* and *The Sh!t No One Tells You*. Reading and watching other parents' stories lets us see that "we're in this together" and gives us a little distance from the fray. It's not just idle distraction to watch your favorite comedy special or sitcom; *laughing is medicine*. Once the dust has settled on a difficult day, you may even want to journal or write about the situation your own family has encountered. Many successful blogs and parenting books have started with nothing but a single, frustrated parent, trying to survive the day with a little bit of humor.

Part II
What to Say to Kids When …

As promised, the rest of this book is devoted to scenarios where we'll have you practice using the framework we shared with you in Chapters 1 and 2. The more you practice, the easier this becomes, but nothing replaces knowing your own kid. That's why we'll provide examples that we've found to be helpful, but it's much more important for you to imagine what's best for you and your child. Once you've surveyed the options, we'll invite you to adapt the model to fit the particular needs of your child and your own unique style.

A couple of last points to ponder before we get started. There have been thousands of parenting books published over many decades. These often fall into two broad categories: managing behavior or helping with feelings. Just focusing on feelings can lead to both parent and child getting stuck on a merry-go-round of emotion; just focusing on behavior can lead to misunderstandings and disconnect. Our hope is to address both aspects, because both are important. It's helpful to think a bit about which half of the equation is your natural comfort zone. If you are someone who feels at home with practical parenting strategies, you'll probably want to pay particular attention to the parts on *building a bridge, emotion translations*, and *putting it into words* to create some balance. If you tend to tune into emotions and talk about feelings with your children more easily and readily, you may want to focus on the sections relating to *getting practical*, including setting limits.

No matter what your leanings as a parent or caregiver, it's universal that kids are more flexible and bounce back more easily when the basics are taken care of. We know that kids melt down more easily when tired, stressed, or hungry. What we sometimes forget to take stock of is the state of their "emotional cup." Kids fill up their cup through connection with the adults who love them. This may be through hugs, playing together, or just spending quality time together. Kids with a full cup will respond even more easily to the practices ahead. But if it's been hard or next to impossible to fill their cup in these ways (maybe even because it's been difficult to be around your child lately), not to worry. The examples in the coming pages will show how you can begin to fill your child's cup even in the midst of the chaos of everyday life and even during your toughest moments together.

Alright! Are you ready? Let's do this!

"I Don't Want to ..." **5**

Let's jump right in with the parenting scenario that is perhaps the most frequently encountered: asking our kids to do something and getting a less than enthusiastic response. When we make requests of our children, they are usually practical demands related to activities of daily living – getting dressed, eating dinner, doing homework, getting to bed. Because what we're asking is so reasonable and necessary, it makes it even more frustrating when our children resist. If we don't want to get stuck in the same old power struggle, we need to try something different. How we respond to their resistance can be a true game-changer.

Scenario A: "I Don't Want to Come for Dinner"

In this scenario, let's assume your child is playing outside with her friends in the neighborhood. When you call her to come in for dinner, she yells back, "I don't want to! I'm not even hungry."

The Knee-Jerk Response

Much of the time, parents and caregivers will respond with something like:

"Come on sweetie, you can go out and play later."

"I worked hard on this meal – let's go!"

Sometimes, especially when frustrated, one might say:

"Too bad! It's time to eat."

Imagine for a moment that your child says to you his or her version of: "I don't want to come for dinner."

What's your most likely knee-jerk response?

_____

_____

_____

 Step 1. Building a Bridge

Imagine you worked in an environment where you were definitely the subordinate employee. Your opinion mattered, but ultimately your superiors got the final say. They decided when you had to work, when you got to take a break – even when and what you ate. That said, you love your job, and most of the time you think your bosses are great. But sometimes it feels frustrating that you don't have more leeway, even if you haven't quite got a handle on the extent of your role. Now let's use this frame of reference to remember what it's like to be a kid and to have to cooperate with umpteen requests per day, from various adults in their life. Children, like adults, want to have some independence. This is a normal human need. Let's also remember how much fun it was to play! As adults, we may no longer have that luxury, but play is what children do. It's their work, their language, their joy, and something they need for their growth and development.

Possible Emotion Translations

Possibility A: "I'm having a lot of fun with my friends!"
Possibility B: "I don't want to miss out on the next game."
Possibility C: "My stomach hasn't given me the signal that I'm hungry yet."

Translations for your child:

_____

_____

_____

*Reminder: If you are feeling stressed, upset or overwhelmed, engaging in this mental exercise can be a real challenge. You might find that taking a break or a couple of deep breaths might make it easier to brainstorm possible emotional translations.

 ## Step 2. Putting It into Words

Option 1. "I don't blame you for not wanting to come in when you're having so much fun."

Option 2. "Dinner is probably the last thing on your mind! Especially that you're just about to start a new game."

Option 3. "I can imagine you want to wait until you're good and hungry before leaving your friends."

In your own words:

I can imagine why you wouldn't want to come in for dinner because _____, and because _____, and because _____.

 ## Step 3. Getting Practical

Emotional support: It makes sense that a child might feel annoyed when asked to stop something he likes doing. Validating his perspective as demonstrated, including acknowledging his frustration, will help. Children need to feel that parents respect their emerging competence – that they are their own people with their own wishes who can start to make some of their own choices. Putting it into words shows that you get this, even though you are still the one setting the schedule and rules for the family. If your child is worried about missing out on something with friends, she might also need reassurance – for example, there will be a next time before too long. Seems simple (and perhaps totally obvious) but when said with sincerity, it can help to make the transition an easier one for your child's brain.

Practical support: Competing with "fun" can be hard. This means that even after you've tried to put it in words and offered reassurance, many children will need you to repeat the request and set a clear limit. When responding to your child in this way (and using this sequence), you may still hear mumbles and grumbles, but it is much more likely that they will be in the house faster and with much less tension, if any.

Next time you need to call your son or daughter for dinner, you may also consider giving a 10-minute warning so that your child can mentally prepare for the upcoming transition. Some kids need a frequent countdown, and some need an adult physically close to help them through transitions. If it's possible to offer them a bit more control over their schedule, once everyone is calm, you can sit down ahead of time and ask them what might work best to help them change tracks. This situation is a great opportunity to work on problem-solving together with your child.

Sample Script: "I Don't Want to Come for Dinner."

PARENT: "Hey sweets, what show are you watching?"

CHILD: (not looking away from the screen) *The Friendly Forest.*

PARENT: "What's going on? It looks like Freda the Fox is being silly."

CHILD: "Yeah, she's pretending to be a dog. She's wagging her tail."

PARENT: "I can see you really like this show. We're having dinner soon, so you'll have to come to the table for dinner in 10 minutes."

CHILD: (whining) "Noooo. I want to watch the rest of the show."

PARENT: "It looks like a good one. Spaghetti doesn't seem as fun as Freda the Fox, now, does it?"

CHILD: (still whining) "No. I want to see what happens next. I want to see why she's trying to be a dog."

PARENT: "I bet you do! It's hard to go from the television to the dinner table, especially when you want to know what's going to happen next! I bet you wish that dinner were later. I'll tell you what, I'll come back in 10 minutes and if the show isn't over, we can pause it so that you can finish watching it after we eat. You can press 'pause' or I can."

CHILD: "Okay, I'm going to press it."

PARENT: "Deal. And we can try to guess over dinner why that silly fox is pretending to be a dog."

Common Pitfalls

1. "He shouldn't need to be told twice." When you tell adults, "It's time to go," they usually get their shoes and coat on and are out the door (okay – most of the time!). Kids move much more slowly, sometimes get distracted, and sometimes get stuck. It actually takes cognitive flexibility for a child to move one from one activity to another, especially since the part of the brain responsible for "shifting sets" is not fully developed until adulthood. Depending on their developmental stage (not their age), it can be harder to do for some kids. This is especially true when the activity to which they are transitioning isn't as "rewarding." Because of this, it's worthwhile to expect a certain degree of resistance as part of a normal interaction when giving a command. When it feels like disrespect, parent and child can get drawn into a standoff where both parties lose flexibility. When you assume your child is stuck rather than just oppositional, it allows you to find more productive ways to help him move forward.

2. "What's the big deal if he stays out longer? I don't want to be controlling." Some of us grew up with military-style discipline and don't want to repeat that for our children. Or we don't want to upset a child who is finally having fun. If it really works for you to let your child have dinner later, there may be no issue; however, when children are able to refuse their parents' requests too often, it can set up a dynamic in which the child is in control. Children feel safer when their parents are in charge and anxious when they aren't, no matter how much they act like they prefer it. Thankfully, when you can validate your child's perspective and stay in charge, it isn't "controlling" but rather teaching and guiding your child to stay on track in a supportive way.

3. "I'm starting to notice that the resistance is mainly around food and mealtimes." Good catch. There are many reasons for hesitancy around eating and mealtimes that don't have to do with just "missing out on fun." Some kids have trouble sitting still at the table, some have sensory issues with foods' tastes or textures, some have anxiety about a part of the eating process, and some may be developing concerns around body image or weight. Along these lines, studies show that 25% of boys and 30% of girls aged 10 to 14 years will experiment with dieting behaviors. Dieting frequently starts in kids as young as 8. In some cases, food resistance persists and can have negative health outcomes for kids. Dieting can lead to increased risk for weight management problems, even eating disorders. If you are worried about your child's eating behaviors, regardless of underlying cause, it is not advised to adopt a "wait and see approach." Rather, check in with your primary care provider to discuss your concerns.

Reflections

What might make it hard for me to put into words my child's experience in a situation like this?

_____

_____

_____

What might make it hard for me to get practical in a situation like this?

_____

_____

_____

What do I need to deal with a situation like this more confidently in the future?

_____

_____

_____

Scenario B: "I Don't Want to Go to bed"

It's bedtime. In some homes, bedtime comes with elaborate plans and strategies, all to avoid a one-way street to meltdown city. Kids resist bedtime for any number of reasons. They may be afraid of the dark, they are still wired from the day, or they may simply have a bad case of FOMO (fear of missing out). In this scenario, when you tell your child it's bedtime, they cry, "Noooooo, I don't want to go to bed!"

The Knee-Jerk Response

Much of the time, parents and caregivers will respond with something like:

"Sorry kiddo – it's that time."

"Honey, you're tired and you need good sleep to be healthy."

Sometimes, especially when frustrated, one might say:

"If you don't get to bed in the next 5 minutes, there's no story and definitely no screen time after dinner tomorrow!"

Imagine for a moment that your child says to you his version of "I don't want to go to bed."

What's your most likely knee-jerk response?

_____

_____

_____

 ## Step 1. Building a Bridge

My kid once shared this with me: "It's not fair that kids have to sleep alone when parents always get to sleep together in the same bed! They always have company!"

How true! I had not crossed the bridge to Child Island in that way before! It is so easy to forget what it's like to be a small kid in a big world where your sense of safety comes from being with your caregivers. Never mind the dark! Easy for us to reassure our children, even lose patience with them, since our brains have since evolved. It's hard to remember what it was actually like to be alone in our bedrooms when our parents were still going about their daily lives without us. The same can be true with kids with older siblings. They often struggle to understand that they have different developmental needs, and so they can feel hurt or offended by the different expectations.

Other children are just too revved up to go to sleep. The child who has lots of energy before bed is no different from how we feel after too much coffee. It can be physically hard to settle down when wired, no matter how tired you are underneath. Kids may anticipate lying in bed feeling jittery, physically uncomfortable, or bored and therefore resist doing so.

Possible Emotion Translations

Possibility A: "I'm scared to be in my room by myself in the dark, and I'm embarrassed to admit it."

Possibility B: "It feels unfair that my sister gets to stay up and I don't. I feel like a baby when I have to go to bed and nobody else does."

Possibility C: "I'm too energetic, and if I go to bed now, I'm just going to feel very bored and very uncomfortable."

Translations for your child:

_____

_____

_____

 ## Step 2. Putting It into Words

Option 1. "Aw – I understand you don't want to go to bed. It can feel a little scary to be upstairs all alone, and that's not a good feeling."

Option 2. "Being the first to bed is hard. I can imagine you don't want to miss out on what we're doing. It probably doesn't feel fair that your sister gets to stay up later."

Option 3. "No wonder you don't want to go to bed, you have so much energy. It feels like we're asking you to flip a switch and suddenly be calm when your body wants to jump around."

In your own words:

I can imagine why you wouldn't want to go to bed right now because _____, and because _____, and because _____.

 ## Step 3. Getting Practical

Emotional support: In general, bedtime can be a great time to connect with your child. It can really help to leave some time, maybe 10 minutes, to engage in connection with your child where the only person in the world that matters to you is her. This kind of connection acts like a fuel for cooperation. Because it can be so hard in our hectic lives to find the time to do so, when you build in this very special ritual in the bedtime routine, your child may actually look forward to getting into bed – or at least they are likely to be far less resistant. If you have more than one kid, 10 minutes may not be possible, but even 2 minutes of special time can help.

Children who are anxious about separation or the dark may also need to feel your confidence in their ability to cope and manage. Once you've validated their feelings, it can be helpful to provide some reassurance – that the room is safe, that you're nearby and will see them in the morning – but there is also a limit on reassurance where it becomes counterproductive. For example, checking once for monsters under the bed can be done in a way that is cute and supportive, but checking twice or three times can fuel the fear.

For the child who is more energetic or disappointed about potentially missing out on the fun, conveying that you get it and that there is always more to look forward to tomorrow can be helpful too.

Practical support: For all kids, routine and consistency can help a lot with bedtime. General principles are the following:

1. Restrict screens for 1 hour before bed.
2. Set the same bedtime every night (ideally on weekends too).
3. Keep a similar routine every night (bath, pajamas, tooth brushing, story, cuddle, etc.).
4. Use a meaningful object (e.g., blanket, stuffed toy) to help child feel more comfortable if sleeping alone.
5. Weave relaxation and mindfulness activities into the routine. The ol' counting sheep strategy can also be a way to calm the busy mind and body.
6. Remember that good sleep is vital to kids' and parents' health and wellbeing. If the child's emotions or behavior are controlling bedtime, then additional strategies will be needed. Please refer to the section on Sleep in Chapter 24: Recommended Readings.

*Reminder: Your ace in the hole is sincerity. Thanks to their mirror neurons, your child's brain will register that your efforts are genuine, leading to a release of calming neurochemicals regardless of how well you follow the structure provided.

Sample Script: "I Don't Want to Go to bed"

PARENT: "Honey! It's bedtime. Get your jammies on, brush your teeth, and I'll be right there to tuck you in."

CHILD: "Aw, can I please stay up for a while longer? We just started a new game."

PARENT: "No sweetie. It's after 8pm already."

CHILD: "You're always ruining our fun. I'm not even tired."

PARENT: "You know, I actually don't blame you for not wanting to go to bed. Adults love to sleep, but most kids don't want to miss out on more fun time at home. Especially since tomorrow means the start of another school day."

CHILD: "Exactly! So why won't you let me stay up later?"

PARENT: "So sorry kiddo. It's time. I promise you'll have more playtime tomorrow."

CHILD: (getting angry) "I don't want to!"

PARENT: "I bet that it's hard to be told what to do all the time, and it can feel lonely in bed, especially when you know Max is still up with us. It might even make you feel like a little kid. Tomorrow after dinner we can sit down and talk about bedtime, but right now I bet you can't beat me up the stairs to the bathroom!"

CHILD: "Fine but I get a head start!"

Common Pitfalls

1. "They just need to go to sleep." Hard to refer to this as a pitfall because it's true. However, if your child has been stuck in a cycle of protesting sleep, he may need some extra support to break that cycle. You may feel that your child shouldn't need external support to get to bed or be concerned he will rely on you for too long. Trust us, kids don't want to go to college with a stuffy, nor do they want their parents to tuck them in forever. It is normal in many societies in the world for children to sleep in bed with their parents for longer than what we consider to be "normal." Humans evolved sleeping together for safety, and our kids' brains are still very much wired for survival. Therefore, kids need to be taught that it's safe to sleep alone, and some kids need a tad bit more of that teaching. And when they get a bit older and feel lonely, they may need to be taught again.

2. "My child is a master at the 'one more thing' strategy." First it's more pages of the story, then a glass of water, then a sore stomach. When kids keep calling you back over and over again, it's enough to drive any parent up the wall. If you're at the end of your rope, it's really important to use the emotion translator so that you can hear what's hidden in your child's repeated requests: "This transition is really hard." As you likely figured out long ago, it's not about the water or the itch; it's about missing you, or worry. If as above you can speak to the feeling: "You're really thirsty, and it's also a bit hard to say goodnight," you can follow this up with a support strategy: "If you miss me at night, you can squeeze Mr. Dog and I'm giving him my special hug to hold just for you." And by all means, set your limit. Nothing fuels frustration like feeling like you have to give in to every demand; it's helpful to be clear about what you will and won't do at bedtime, and remember that your calm and confident approach to your child is what's most helpful.

Reflections

What might make it hard for me to put into words my child's experience in a situation like this?

_____

_____

_____

What might make it hard for me to get practical in a situation like this?

_____

_____

_____

What do I need to deal with a situation like this more confidently in the future?

_____

_____

_____

Scenario C. "I Don't Want to Do My homework"

In this next "I don't want to …" scenario, let's assume it's time for homework. Your son really struggles with reading, and that's what's on tonight's agenda. You're already dreading it. It's always a battle, and you're worried he's going to have a really negative relationship with reading, even homework in general. When you ask him to get his book out, he responds, "I don't want to! The teacher gave us the dumbest book."

The Knee-Jerk Response

Much of the time, parents and caregivers will respond with something like:

"I'm sure it's not that bad. The sooner you get through your chapter, the sooner you can move on to something else."

"Honey, you are doing SO well. You get better all the time but you need to keep practicing."

Sometimes, especially when frustrated, one might say:

"Don't be rude. Your teacher works hard to support your learning. No book is dumb."

Imagine for a moment that your child says to you her version of "I don't want to do my homework."

What's your most likely knee-jerk response?

_____

_____

_____

 Step 1. Building a Bridge

There are many reasons a child may not want to read. Children develop reading skills at different paces, and sometimes the material is just too difficult for them at that time. For children with language-based learning differences, reading can feel like asking them to build a bridge. There are so many invisible components to the task, and it's easy to get overwhelmed without the proper supports. And imagine being asked to perform a difficult task in front of other people (even your parents); children can feel a lot of embarrassment at the prospect of letting on that something is hard for them, especially if "everyone else" can do it just fine. Other children struggle with attention span, sitting still and focusing on a less preferred activity. Even at the best of times and with no underlying cognitive issues, reading and other school tasks require mental energy and the enjoyment develops over time.

Possible Emotion Translations

Possibility A: "When I struggle to read, it makes me feel really bad about myself and I don't want to feel that way."

Possibility B: "The content of the book doesn't reflect my interests, so it's hard to stay focused."

Possibility C: "My brain is tired after a long day at school, so the idea of doing something mentally challenging sounds painful."

Translations for your child:

_____

_____

_____

⬭ Step 2. Putting It into Words

Option 1. "I can understand why you wouldn't want to dive in. Reading is not your favorite subject, and so I imagine it's not a lot of fun."

Option 2. "I bet you're not excited to read about more farm animals; it's too bad the book isn't about motorcycles."

Option 3. "I can imagine that after a long day, the thought of reading for homework is tiring."

In your own words:

I can imagine why you wouldn't want to do your reading homework because _____, and because _____, and because _____.

*Reminder: This step is most effective when you can use one of the sentence starters followed by three because-statements that reflect why it might make sense for your child to feel, think or act this way.

Step 3. Getting Practical

Emotional support: Kids (and all people for that matter) want to be valued for who they are. When they feel they aren't living up to expectations, they can feel embarrassed or fear rejection. This is why it's crucial to keep the parent–child relationship positive with patience and encouragement while working on homework (e.g., "you've worked through projects before and I'm sure we can do this together"). We know this is a tall order, yet as soon as kids sense criticism and disappointment, they are likely to shut down or want to avoid homework even more than they already did in the first place. The need here is also for acceptance of where the child is at rather than pressure to be where we want him to be. The child struggling with reading or homework also needs our confidence that he will learn and grow, as all children do.

Practical support: In this scenario and others like it, getting practical might involve some support in moving through the task. There are many practical ways to support your child with homework, one of which is to use what is referred to as a *scaffolding technique* (in the same way scaffolding is used around a building under construction). This means the parents or caregivers provide just enough support that children can complete the task without the adult taking over fully or doing for them what they can do for themselves. For example, a parent may demonstrate how to solve a problem or read a word, and then they step back to allow their child to give it a try. Or a parent may let their child come up with the ideas for a project but help spell the words. In some cases, reading instructions aloud to the child, helping to organize the steps, or scribing their answers may be necessary to support the child to complete the task.

Parents can also help by structuring homework time. For example, you can spend some connecting time with kids after school before homework (e.g., playing a game) and then set a timer for short bursts of focused homework time with movement breaks in between. "I'll set the timer for 15 minutes and after that we'll turn on the music and dance for 5 minutes before getting back to work again."

Because it is such hard work to be a parent and homework helper at the same time, it may be more practical to work with a good tutor or advocate for extra help at school if the resources are available. You may even consider enlisting a teen from the neighborhood who needs volunteer hours or grandparents, aunts and uncles. This may be especially relevant for children with learning differences who may require extra support to help them reach their potential.

Sample Script: "I Don't Want to Do My Homework"

PARENT: "Time to do your math homework!"

CHILD: "Ugh, I'll do it later."

PARENT: "I don't blame you for not wanting to do it. Word problems are not easy, especially at the end of a long day."

CHILD: "It's stupid. I swear I'm never going to use this stuff."

PARENT: "It is extra hard to feel motivated to do something that's tough *and* feels like a waste of time."

CHILD: "Plus you're always nagging me about it."

PARENT: "Yeah, I know, it makes it worse when we get into it with each other. On top of the work, we get into battles, which doesn't feel good. No wonder you don't want to get going."

CHILD: "See! If I didn't do homework, we wouldn't fight! Problem solved!"

PARENT: "Yeah, it would be awesome if there were never any homework. I feel for you, kiddo. I really do. And I know you can get this over and done with before too long. Do you want to tackle it on your own or do you want to look at the book with me first?"

CHILD: "I'll just start."

PARENT: "You got it. I'll come check on you in a few."

Common Pitfalls

1. "**If I validate how hard math can be, won't he avoid the subject?**"
When your child struggles with a school subject, it can be scary to put that struggle into words in case it somehow makes it more likely that they will shy away from academics in general. Parents usually take on the role of cheerleader (you've got this!) or enforcer (you've got to do this!) instead. Thankfully you can breathe easy knowing that responding in the ways we've suggested here will actually decrease your child's resistance, increase his engagement, and therefore, his skill and confidence. It's also important for kids to know their own personal profile of strengths and weaknesses. One of the ways you can support your child to develop healthy school-based self-esteem is to help him to celebrate his gifts and feel okay about his difficulties.

2. "What if she never succeeds in school?" Kids spend the majority of their time in school, and so much can feel like it's riding on school performance: their self-esteem, peer group, acceptance to college/university, career. It's a lot of pressure on parents to choose the right schools and programs and to help kids do their very best. When a child is struggling with academics, this rubs up against one of parenting's basic unwritten rules: Don't let your child do poorly in school! Some of us blame ourselves for the problems or get really frustrated at our kids that they aren't trying harder or doing better. Fundamentally, this goes back to not wanting to see them suffer and worrying about a future which doesn't yet exist, in which we imagine them living below their potential. It can also feel embarrassing to see one's child fall short of our expectations or what we imagine society's expectations to be. This is one of those situations where we need to find a way to shelve the worry or shame and remember that the inherent nature of all children is to develop, learn, and grow. Once we can get our own worries out of the way, it frees us up to continue accompanying them on their path and supporting them in the best way we can.

Reflections

What might make it hard for me to put into words my child's experience in a situation like this?

_____

_____

_____

What might make it hard for me to get practical in a situation like this?

_____

_____

_____

What do I need to deal with a situation like this more confidently in the future?

_____

_____

_____

"I Miss ..." 6

With grief and loss, regardless of age, there really isn't a statute of limitations on how long you can be affected. The expectation that we should "get over" a loss, doesn't fit with human experience, even if the loss we are experiencing appears trivial to others. For example, before I owned a pet, I did not understand how absolutely devastating this kind of loss could be (and for how long!). We may adapt, but the loss remains a part of our lives. Grief can come in waves and also be tied with other feelings like anger and regret. Kids may sometimes show fewer external signs of grief or signs like anxiety and behavioral changes that are less recognizable. They may also be highly affected by the loss of someone they didn't seem particularly close to, especially if their main caregivers are grieving.

Scenario A: "I Miss Rosie!"

It's been 1 year since the death of your family dog. She was an important figure in your life, and the transition has been difficult for everyone. Whenever your child is upset, she bursts into tears, exclaiming: "I miss Rosie!"

The Knee-Jerk Response

Parents and caregivers will often respond with something like:

"Of course you do, but she's in a better place now. Let's focus on that."

"Honey, are you sure that's what you're upset about?"

Sometimes, especially when frustrated, one might say:

"I'm really sorry but crying isn't going to bring her back."

Imagine for a moment that your child says to you her version of "I miss Rosie!"

What's your most likely knee-jerk response?

_____

_____

_____

 Step 1. Building a Bridge

Children often come to understand death or loss differently with every few years, as they mature. For example, a child under 7 likely doesn't understand the permanence of death. A 10-year-old starts to make the connection that if any creature dies, all creatures, including family members, will eventually die too. If a parent gets ill, is injured, or away more often, this can also create worry and insecurity for the child that they can't yet understand or articulate. Children can also have bonds with pets or family members that adults aren't fully aware of. For example, after a divorce, a family dog may be the one who travels back and forth between homes with the child, becoming the most constant companion in her life.

Possible Emotion Translations

Possibility A: "The pain of the loss is still so big, I can hardly handle it. Please help me to move through this feeling."

Possibility B: "I'm so upset. When I used to feel bad, Rosie was always there to pet. I know you love me, but it's not the same."

Possibility C: "Now that I've learned about death, I'm worried about *you* dying. The thought of that is too much to handle."

Translations for your child:

_____

_____

_____

Step 2. Putting It into Words

Option 1. "It is so hard to think about Rosie because there's still so much sadness that comes with the thoughts – like a humongous wave inside your body."

Option 2. "Rosie was a great friend. It's so hard to go through stuff like this without her."

Option 3. "Since we lost Rosie, I wonder if you might even be worried about losing me."

In your own words:

I can imagine why you'd feel sad about Rosie because _____, and because _____, and because _____.

*Reminder: Although these statements are meant to calm the storm in the brain, we don't want to stop there. If we did, it could feel like a bit of a cliffhanger. It's once you've spoken their perspective that your child be more open to your emotional and practical support.

 ## Step 3. Getting Practical

Emotional support: This comes pretty intuitively to parents – when kids are grieving, what they need is comfort, comfort, and more comfort. It helps to allow and even encourage the expression of sadness, confusion and fear, if you think they are present. We can never reassure kids fully that nothing bad will ever happen to those they love, but we can put it in a realistic context and make sure kids know they will never be alone. Kids may also need to know that they are not to somehow at fault, because they may hold onto a version of events in which they blame themselves (this happens to adults too!). They may also need to know that it's okay (and normal) to feel mad when faced with loss. You can draw on your family's own spiritual beliefs for these discussions and share whatever comfort they may provide. And with all of this, it may need to be done in small doses so the child can handle it. A child may only tolerate a few minutes of talking about a loss and then be eager to get out and play. There is no need to expect a child to sit in feelings of grief for longer than he can. He will come back to them over time in a way he can manage, as long as you are open to it or initiating the opportunities to circle back once in a while.

Practical support: First, kids generally benefit from talking about death in a straightforward, developmentally appropriate manner. Rituals, like celebrations of life, funerals, and marking anniversaries, can be important to help the child feel they are not alone in their grief and to make meaning of the loss. Children may not fully understand what has happened, yet they are very sensitive to the grief of adults around them, and they will likely sense that something major has happened, whether you tell them all of the details or not. It is usually better to have some explanation and participation in rituals than to be alone with the mystery and fear of feeling something is wrong but having no idea what it is.

Sample Script: "I Miss Rosie!"

CHILD: "I miss Rosie!"

PARENT: "Aw, Rosie was a really special dog."

CHILD: (sobbing) "I want her to come hoooooome."

PARENT: "Of course you do, honey. Rosie was like your protector. And she was such a good friend to you. I bet that the world just doesn't feel quite right without her."

CHILD: (sobbing) "She was my *best* friend!"

PARENT: (wrapping her up in a big hug) "And it's really hard to believe that you won't be able to give her hugs anymore or play fetch or even pick up her stinky poop."

CHILD: "Don't make jokes. It's not funny."

PARENT: "You're right, of course it's not funny. I'm sorry honey. Losing a pet is one of the hardest things to go through, even for adults. The sadness is so big. It can feel like a big wave that knocks you over and that's really hard."

CHILD: (sniffling) "I'm really sad and mad and I just want her back."

PARENT: (squeezing a little tighter) "It is really sad and it feels really unfair. I'll tell you what – let's draw a picture of Rosie to put on the refrigerator. You know how much she loved hanging out in the kitchen."

CHILD: (giggling) "Yeah, she just wanted to steal our food."
PARENT: "She sure did that little sneaky girl. Then, let's go for a walk down her favorite trail. I think that will help a lot."

Common Pitfalls

1. "We've been through this so many times already." When children suffer a serious loss (of a pet or a family member), they may ask the same or similar questions over and over again. If they are younger, they may also get lost in their sadness. In these instances, it is important to answer their questions as directly as possible, validate their feelings (using because-statements), and offer comfort, and then transition to offering practical support through your presence and refocusing on the present moment. If the grief feels stuck, there may be parts of the loss your child still hasn't shared, like the fact that he blames himself, even if this is irrational. Self-blame in the context of loss is incredibly common – even among adults – and so a good idea to check it out just in case.

2. "I don't think it's really about the dog anymore." It is possible that children use the loss of a pet or family member to discharge sadness in general, especially if they worry that expressing vulnerability might be regarded as a weakness or inappropriate. If your spidey-senses are going off, you can also speak what you believe to be the "unspoken": "I wonder if Rosie is helping you to talk about other things you're feeling sad about – like how much you miss Daddy tonight. It would be totally normal if you did. Just in case, let me give you an extra squeeze and see if we can't get him on the phone for a few minutes before bedtime."

3. "Won't a new dog help him move on?" If you felt compelled to bring a new dog into the family to ease your child's suffering, you're not alone. It's the ultimate fix. Although it can be a wonderful experience to introduce a new pet, it can't be at the exclusion of addressing the pain of the loss. In fact, attending to the loss *before* getting a new pet ensures that your child's experience of grief won't be interrupted by the distraction and he can process his feelings fully with your support. If there is already a new pet, it's still not too late to honor remaining feelings about the loss of the previous pet.

Reflections

What might make it hard for me to put into words my child's experience in a situation like this?

_____

_____

_____

What might make it hard for me to get practical in a situation like this?

_____

_____

_____

What do I need to deal with a situation like this more confidently in the future?

_____

_____

_____

Scenario B: "I Miss Our Old Place!"

Imagine you got a great job, but it's in a neighboring city and so you decide to move homes to avoid a lengthy commute. Your child has to go to a new school and say goodbye to neighborhood friends. For the past 4 months since you moved, your child complains nonstop about the decision. Today is an especially loud outburst of "I miss our old place!"

The Knee-Jerk Response

Much of the time, parents and caregivers will respond with something like:

"Honey, we needed to move for my job, and you have a way bigger bedroom now."

"I know, kiddo. It's a good thing there are a lot of new kids to play with in this neighborhood. You'll have even more friends now!"

Sometimes, especially when frustrated, one might say:

"You'll just have to get used to it! We all have to make sacrifices."

Imagine for a moment that your child says to you his version of "I miss our old place!"

What's your most likely knee-jerk response?

_____

_____

_____

 ## Step 1. Building a Bridge

If you're a parent of a school-age child, you know that social relationships are incredibly important to children. Studies even show that they are essential to a child's well-being, including their sense of satisfaction in life. Having to say goodbye to friends or even just seeing them less often can have a big impact on a child's mood. Children usually understand all the practical reasons for a move, but they have no control over it. Even positive changes cause stress for most people.

Possible Emotion Translations

Possibility A: "I know that I'll make new friends, but it's just not the same without my old ones. We grew up together and I don't have to worry about trying to impress them. It's so much easier to just be myself."

Possibility B: "Even if I get to see my old friends at school, I still miss going to the corner store together and playing in the tree house. We can't do those things at recess. Plus, I'm worried they'll forget about me or replace me with someone new."

Possibility C: "I still miss my old room, and our old sofa. I'm worried you'll think that's stupid or childish, so I don't say anything about these things."

Translations for your child:

_____

_____

_____

 **Step 2. Putting It into Words**

Option 1. "Moving was hard for all kinds of reasons but maybe most of all because you don't get to see your friends as often as you would like. It's a pain to get on your bike or organize a ride there and back when before you could just run out the front door to see them."

Option 2. "I can imagine you feel really sad about having to change schools. I wonder if you're feeling a little mad at us for buying a house across town. Maybe you feel like we didn't think about how hard it would be for you."

Option 3. "I bet you wish things could have just stayed the same. After all, this wasn't your choice and now it's hard to fit in. I'd be pretty mad too if I were in your shoes."

In your own words:
I can imagine why you'd feel upset about moving because _____, and because _____, and because _____.

*Reminder: The idea here is to connect with your child's good intentions, vulnerable feelings, or need for connection driving his or her current state of being, even if on the surface it doesn't seem so.

 Step 3. Getting Practical

Emotional support: This scenario is also about loss, even though it may come out as frustration or even criticism toward the parent. This child needs acceptance that it's okay to be angry and upset about the move and to have the underlying pain acknowledged. There will also be a need for comfort and connection because the ground can feel shaky after a major life change. In fact, kids may also want you around more after a big move. This is normal, and doesn't mean they are becoming overly anxious. We all need more comfort and reassurance from our main people when things around us are changing a lot.

Practical support: As all the changes and potential losses are acknowledged, it becomes easier to help your child to start thinking about all the exciting new elements of your life. A kid who is screaming "We never should have moved anyway!" isn't ready or able to hear about the bigger newer park or the higher quality school. That said, once she's feeling understood, she will likely want help to reorient her thinking toward the positives and the ways she can adapt to her new environment. The child may also need practical support to maintain connections with old friends. For example, as savvy as kids are online, they may need advice and some encouragement to reach out to old friends or transportation for play dates. Kids who are shyer may also need some support from parents to invite new kids to the house. All it takes is one friend with whom they feel comfortable to make life at school manageable, but sometimes making that first friend can take a lot of effort.

Sample Script: "I Miss Our Old Place!"

CHILD: "I can't hang out with my friends. I hate that we moved. Why did you and Dad have to be so selfish? I hate this house and this neighborhood, and there's nothing to do."

PARENT: "I can understand why you'd feel that way. Your friends were your world and we turned that upside down, didn't we?"

CHILD: "I hate it here."

PARENT: "I bet. Life was a lot easier back at the old house. You could just run outside and at any given time and one of your buddies would be ready to play."

CHILD: "Or just hang out. I'm not a little kid anymore."

PARENT: "Right. Or just hang out. And now it's different and the kids are different – they've got their own thing going on. If I were you, I might even feel a little awkward trying to find my way in the neighborhood."

CHILD: "It is awkward."

PARENT: "I'm sorry, bud. I don't blame you for being mad at us. You miss your old pack. Even though they are a drive away, it's just not the same, and chances are it never will be."

CHILD: "Whoa. It's not *that* bad."

PARENT: "Right – I overdid it there."

CHILD: "It just sucks."

PARENT: "Of course. And in the meantime, let me know if you want to organize an afternoon back at the old place."

CHILD: "Sure. You can leave now."

PARENT: "Roger that. You've had enough. Okay – just know that dinner is in 15."

Common Pitfalls

1. "Maybe I shouldn't have accepted the new job." You may be feeling really badly about the impact the move had on your child, especially if it was long distance. If you're suffering with guilt or regret, it may make it hard to take the complaint from your child because it just makes you feel worse. It may help to remember that your child's distress is temporary and colored by the lens of not being able to see the "bigger picture." Life can be hard, and luckily, when it comes to emotional adaptation, it's not what happens, it's how it's handled. Focus on kindness to yourself and maybe grieving what you've left behind as well. It will get easier to venture into your child's own sadness and sense of loss.

2. "I don't get it. Up until today, she seemed totally fine." Perhaps your child acts cool as a cucumber, and it's a total surprise that she's upset all of a sudden. For example, your child might avoid talking about her friends or even insist that she is just fine. In this case, it's harder to build the bridge, and you'll need to make an educated guess that she isn't necessarily fine but may be putting on a brave face. You can still put into words her perspective, which in this case is that you can understand why she would want to distance herself from the pain or pretend the old friends never existed "because … because … because …" (e.g., because moving away from friends can really hurt!). Validating your child's resistance to talk about her painful feelings can help to open the door for her to talk about the more vulnerable feelings she has inside. More on this topic in Chapter 10 ("I'm Not Talking to You …").

Reflections

What might make it hard for me to put into words my child's experience in a situation like this?

_____

_____

_____

What might make it hard for me to get practical in a situation like this?

_____

_____

_____

What do I need to deal with a situation like this more confidently in the future?

_____

_____

_____

Figure 6.1 The knee-jerk response

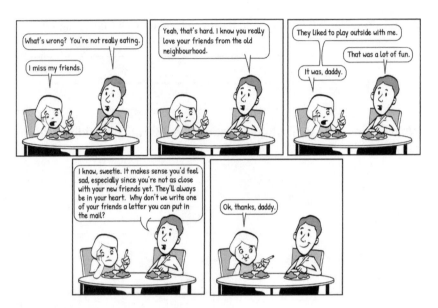

Figure 6.2 Validation and support

"You Love My Sister More …"   **7**

Moving on to a doozy for parents of more than one kid or who are part of a blended family. If that's you, chances are you've heard some version of "You love _____ more."

A similar version is "How come _____ gets to do _____ when I don't?" We often think of sibling rivalry as an issue between siblings, but it's also an issue between parent and child. This isn't just because the conflict affects parents; the rivalry is usually over some aspect of the parents' love, attention, or resources. This example is a classic scenario in which engaging the emotion translator is just as important as putting your child's experience into words and offering support.

Scenario: "You Love My Sister More …"

Imagine that your daughter has had a rough semester, and so you set aside some special time together, including a shopping trip one evening. You've had a great time together, and you're both in a good mood. When you walk in the door, your son sees you together, then makes a comment about the time you've spent with his sister lately and how she can stay out longer. He then asks, "Do you love Sam more?"

The Knee-Jerk Response

Much of the time, parents and caregivers will respond with something like:

"Of course not, sweetie. I love you both the same. You'll see when you become a parent."

"We do so much together; I'm not sure how you can ask that."

Sometimes, especially when frustrated, one might say:

"Well, she doesn't give me a hard time as often as you do."

Imagine for a moment that your child says to you her version of "You love my sister more …"

What's your most likely knee-jerk response?

_____

_____

_____

 ## Step 1. Building a Bridge

When we build a bridge to Child Island, we may find that our child is picking up on subtle (or not so subtle) differences in the ways we interact with other members of the family, regardless of whether this is justified – say in the case of a sibling with special needs. And if one of your daughters is more "like" you, no doubt you will "get her" more easily. You will be better able to guess what she is thinking and how she is feeling in a variety of situations. The same won't necessarily be true for this child who may resemble your co-parent or who walks to the beat of his own drum. As a result, you will sometimes struggle to understand why he reacts in the ways he sometimes does. When it comes to quality time together, if you and your daughter both enjoy shopping, relating to one another can be effortless. On the other hand, if your son is into video games and that is just not your cup of tea, you may struggle to connect in a way that is meaningful for him. In other words, our children are on to something! But their lack of sophistication to understand the bigger picture makes it so they use very rudimentary means to communicate that they are picking up on something that leaves them feeling bad.

Possible Emotion Translations

Possibility A. "I feel sad when I see how easily you get along with my sister. It hurts me that we can't get on as effortlessly."

Possibility B. "I feel left out when you spend time with my sister. It's hard for me to admit that because I know she needs you too."

Possibility C: "I'm hurt that you don't seem to have as much fun playing my games. I also can't understand why she's allowed to do a lot more than I can."

Translations for your child:

_____

_____

_____

Step 2. Putting It into Words

Option 1. "I can see how you might feel that way because your sister and I have a lot in common: shopping, makeup, getting our hair done. And you and I are really different, so it can feel like we are less connected at times."

Option 2. "I can imagine that when you see how much time I give to your sister it tells you that she's more important. It doesn't matter what the reasons are – it still hurts."

Option 3. "Your perspective makes sense to me. You see her getting to stay out later and you aren't allowed yet. No wonder you feel like I love her more. Like if I loved you as much, then I'd let you stay out later too".

In your own words:

I can imagine why you would feel like I love your sister more because _____, and because _____, and because _____.

 ## Step 3. Getting Practical

Emotional support: No matter how your child communicates his fear that you don't love him as much as another child (or even your partner), the emotional is need is always a vulnerable one. Now that you've spoken his perspective and he can actually hear your supportive words, it's time to put his experience in context and address any misperceptions. Something like this can go a long way: "You need to know that I love you with every ounce of my being," topped off with the identification of something unique and special about that child, like this: "I especially love how bold you are, and I admire your outgoing personality. You really remind me how important it is to get out there and have fun."

Practical support: The practical need in this scenario is to make a concerted effort to increase 1:1 connection time, even if for brief moments, although a special date night can go a long way to transform the hurt. It can also be cool for kids to have you join them in the activities they really like, especially when they know you don't:

> I am going to make an effort for us to spend more quality time together. And we'll do some of the things you like to do – even play video games together – so that I can get to know you and your interests better.

I worked with a set of parents who often made negative comments about their son's video-game playing – they really wanted him to know the downsides of his new hobby – but it created disconnect between them. And so you can imagine his surprise when they asked to play with him! He had such a riot teaching them game play strategies, and they were careful to focus on the positive aspects of the experience. Simple but powerful.

Sample Script: "You Love My Sister More …"

CHILD: "Mom, do you love Ellie more than me?"
PARENT: "Hmm, that's a big question, sweetie. I wonder if you're asking because I've been spending more time with her lately?"
CHILD: "Well, do you?"
PARENT: "Honey, I can understand why you might feel like I love Ellie more because I've been helping her with her homework almost every night, and you and I haven't had the same amount of cuddle time we usually do."
CHILD: "Well, yeah …"

PARENT: "And I bet that feels pretty yucky, because our cuddle time is some of the only 'me-and-you' time we get in a day. You might be thinking to yourself that maybe I've forgotten about you or that I don't care as much about our special time together."

CHILD: "Yeah."

PARENT: "Aw, that's a terrible feeling, to feel like your mom is too busy or doesn't care. I'm so glad you told me."

CHILD: "You are?"

PARENT: "Yes, for sure. When I put myself in your shoes, your feelings make a lot of sense, and so I really get to see what needs to be done."

CHILD: "What's that?"

PARENT: "Well first of all, I have to remind you of how much I love you. Like to the moon and back and back again and back again a hundred more times."

CHILD: (giggles)

PARENT: Also, I have to make more of an effort to make sure our special time happens. And if for whatever reason we have to miss a night or cut it short, I'm going to check in with you to see if you need another reminder or just a big ol' squeeze. Like this! (gives her a bear hug)

CHILD: (giggles again) "Okay!"

Common Pitfalls

1. "She's just saying that to get what she wants." It's true that kids may want something and say things more dramatically to get it, but a kid who says "You love my sister more!" is usually asking for more connection with the parent, not attention in a random way. In fact, we urge parents to consider revising the statement: "attention-seeking" to "connection-seeking" – it's far more accurate and will help you to lead with compassion instead of annoyance. Sure, kids can go about expressing their need in clunky or off-putting ways, but it's important to validate what's there so that you can uncover the deeper feelings under this more surface level complaint. If it's still hard to speak *her* perspective (remember, her brain is still immature, and so her interpretations will be too), go back to *building a bridge*. It may also be that something in her comment is upsetting you, and it's getting in the way of your ability to see the situation from where she sits. Check in with yourself and take those few breaths to see if that helps.

2. "I always seem to get it wrong!" Maybe your child shuts you down or communicates some other protest when you try to put into words their perspective. We have to remember that while we're making educated guesses, we can't read our child's mind. So we can validate this too: "It sounds like I was way off base. And I bet that makes it feel even worse. It's really important for you that I get you and it hurts when I don't" (more on that topic in Chapter 12: "You Just Don't Get It!"). It may also be that your child responds this way because what you said is bang on. And by touching into the pain, it gives your child a bit of a shock that makes it so that they reflexively "blast" you. That's actually a good sign as it signals a release, and so a good idea is to remain calm and connected until the wave passes.

3. "What if I have to deal with both of them at the same time?" In families with more than one child, other kids may be around while you're having these conversations. As soon as you direct your attention to one child and put into words his experience, the other may react and pipe up to say something like "It's not my fault my homework takes so long!" That sibling may feel guilty for taking the parents' time or resentful because they don't feel like they are getting enough quality time either. In this kind of situation, you may need to validate one child's experience and then turn and do the same for the other child(ren), cycling back and forth a few times. We refer to this as "validation whack-a-mole." It may even work well to have a full family discussion where you can talk openly about everyone's feelings so they don't carry around guilt or resentment under the radar. This is especially important if one or more child has an illness or disability that requires a lot of the family's resources in an ongoing way.

*Reminder: The proposed framework is not a magic formula. It can also feel really awkward since it goes against so much of what we were taught about how to respond to children's thoughts and feelings. We do urge you to try it out a few times following the steps as closely as possible as practice really does make a difference over time.

Reflections

What might make it hard for me to put into words my child's experience in a situation like this?

_____

_____

_____

What might make it hard for me to get practical in a situation like this?

_____

_____

_____

What do I need to deal with a situation like this more confidently in the future?

_____

_____

_____

"This Is the BEST!" 8

This chapter is a little different from the others because the child isn't upset – instead she may be happy, excited, or overjoyed. We wouldn't typically think of this as a difficult moment, yet for many of us, responding to joy doesn't come naturally. We may have been conditioned to downplay our child's excitement (e.g., don't be braggy!) or we see the potential downsides of its expression (e.g., leading to jealousy in a sibling or a "too big" expression in public) or we may not understand nor approve of the reason for it (e.g., I just leveled up in my game!). Who knew joy could be so complicated?

Enjoying and celebrating joy with others is one of the most connecting experiences people can have, and yet it can be an incredibly difficult emotion to sustain. This is especially true as we get older and are influenced by external messaging about outward expressions of joy and happiness. Have you ever witnessed something really cool and looked right around to see with whom you could relate? Joy becomes buoyant when it is shared; when there's no one, it can feel like the bubble deflates, even bursts. When the people we care about ignore our joy, invalidate it or don't share in it, it can even lead to a sudden shift in our experience from joy to sadness, anger, even shame. We can then end up focusing on these negative states. The number one reason to get "good" at joy? It has the capacity to spread far and wide, bringing more joy into our family's life too.

Scenario A: "This Is the BEST!"

Imagine your 11-year-old daughter comes running to you holding her tablet and says: "This is the BEST! My favorite YouTuber just posted three new crafting videos!!! Eeeeeeeeee!"

The Knee-Jerk Response

Much of the time, parents and caregivers will respond with something like:

(Flatly) "That's great honey."

"Okay, just remember you only have 10 minutes left of screen time."

Sometimes, especially when frustrated, one might say:

"Too loud! If you like these videos so much why don't you just craft yourself!"

Imagine for a moment that your child says to you her version of "This Is the BEST!"

What's your most likely knee-jerk response?

_____

_____

_____

 ## Step 1. Building a Bridge

Think about how excited your child got about balloons or ice cream or toy trucks when he was really little. Wasn't it adorable? As children get older, they convey their excitement by jumping up and down or telling you a million details about something. The problem is that we all have different interests and things that we're passionate about. What they find exciting may be neutral, boring, or even irritating to us. They may also be taking up a lot of space in their expression – something our culture has taught us is a no-no. The joy for them is untainted by adult awareness of the supposed downsides. To reconnect with our primary instincts around joy, it helps to harness the youthful excitement and wonder you felt about something as a child. We often get trained out of unrestrained joy as adults, so remembering childlike joy can be really helpful.

Possible Emotion Translations

Possibility A: "I'm so excited to learn from these videos. It makes me feel so proud to create new worlds."

Possibility B: "I'm so happy to finally get more of my favorite thing and I want to share my joy with you."

Possibility C: "It feels so good to be happy and when you're happy for me too – it's even better."

Translations for your child:

_____

_____

_____

Step 2. Putting It into Words

Option 1. "Three new videos! You've been waiting for these for a long time, and you love crafting so much; no wonder you're over the moon!"

Option 2. "Yippee!!!! I see why you're so happy, because she is your absolute favorite in the world and now you get to watch even more of her awesome tips!"

Option 3. "This IS the BEST! High-five girl! So happy for you!"

In your own words:

I can imagine why you would be so excited because _____, and because _____, and because _____.

*A note for joy: This step is most effective when you can embody your child's joy – in other words – when your words and your body convey understanding of their experience. It doesn't mean you need to jump up on the couch to show you get it, but a little extra energy and animation can go a long way.

 ## Step 3. Getting Practical

Emotional support: Simply put – joy wants to be joined! A happy kid wants to connect with you and share the joy. Your connection sustains the experience, even heightens it, and we could all use a little more joy as armor against the challenges of life. The added bonus – smiles are contagious; let yourself catch them! This creates a real sense of togetherness and mutual enjoyment. Studies show that sharing positive experiences leads to more happiness and satisfaction with life overall – even more energy (although we may not really want our kids to have more energy some days ☺). When in addition to sharing the experience, we also receive encouraging, enthusiastic, and positive messages, we are more likely to experience even more happiness, love, and gratitude.

Practical support: Enjoying your child's joy and making space for her to experience it is plenty! If you have the energy to take it to the next level, showing interest in your child's passion ("Let me see!" or "Oh cool – how does she do that!") conveys your support for her pursuing what she loves. It can be really cool if you then ask your child to teach you something from this arena. If it's something you don't enjoy, then no need to pretend, just focus on positive curiosity ("I wonder what she'll have up her sleeve next?").

Sample Script: "This Is the BEST!"

CHILD: (excitedly) "Dad, I have the BEST news: Jake and I are going to start a podcast!"

PARENT: (with enthusiasm) "No way! That's really cool."

CHILD: "Seriously! We're going to interview other kids from school about stuff and post it."

PARENT: "That must be so exciting for you guys. You've always loved talking to people and you've wanted to be on radio or TV since you were little!"

CHILD: "Yep. This is the first step, Dad. And Jake's really funny. We already have three friends who said yes to being interviewed."

PARENT: "Nice. Good for you guys! Already three people! So cool that kids will have content made by kids. You're really working on this! I bet that feels really exciting."

CHILD: "We are, Dad!!"

PARENT: "Are you going to start with a certain topic or just see how the interview goes?"

CHILD: "We don't know yet. We're going to ask around to see what people want to hear about. I have a couple of ideas already though."

PARENT: "Oh – I can't wait to hear them! The only thing we do need to talk about is privacy stuff and how to get proper permission to post about other people, especially since they're kids. I can help with that part."

CHILD: "Okay. I guess that's fine. You can be our 'assistant.'"

PARENT: "Ha. Fair enough. You guys are the directors and I'll get your coffee."

CHILD: (smiling) "That's right!"

Common Pitfalls

1. "What if I don't agree with the thing he's happy about?" No parent can or should fake happiness. Just like with all the other emotions, understanding, accepting, and reflecting the *feelings* doesn't mean agreeing with the *behaviors*. Let's take a more extreme example: Let's say your daughter was to come home excited about her desire to get a piercing. We would never say you have to agree to it because it makes her happy, nor do you need to pretend you're happy about her desire to get a piercing. What we're proposing is that you can acknowledge her happiness with something like: "I can imagine why you'd be so happy about it, because it would be something that's yours and because it will make you feel good every time you look at it." You can still limit or say "no" to what your child enjoys, and if you do, the validation you've offered on the front end will soften the blow. The truth is, we can't change what other people feel happy about nor can we change our own feelings, but we can see the positive intentions behind our child's motivations and communicate this to them so that they feel respected and understood.

2. "I don't want him to be disappointed." As adults, many of us have lost some of our idealism. We want to protect our kids from pain and disappointment. We may believe that it's better to dampen their enthusiasm proactively rather than see them hurt later. That's why parents often express caution in the face of joy ("don't get your hopes up") or jump to getting practical ("but realistically, how are you ever going to that?"). The downside is that cautioning usually makes the child feel less creative and adventurous. Children want their parents to believe in them. It is through this belief that they develop more belief in themselves. When you can join in their joy, children are more likely to feel confident. They are also likely to be more receptive to your emotional and practical support, including the good advice you have to offer.

3. "I was always taught humility. I don't want her joy to be hurtful or off-putting to others!" This is a really good point. We agree that humility is a crucial value. Some parents have also shared that they feel anxious when one of their kids expresses "big" joy in case it triggers bad feelings in another. For example, a child might be super excited about an invitation to a party in front of a sibling who hasn't yet found her tribe. It's really difficult to simultaneously join in your child's joy and be sensitive to your other child's pain, and often, joy gets the cut. In this scenario, you might choose to celebrate first with your joyful child and then connect one-to-one with the other later so that both their needs can be met.

A final note on joy: Do you ever feel like too much joy is frivolous, unproductive, or self-indulgent? If so – join the club. There are deep historical roots to the suppression of joy. Some scholars believe that joy blocks date back to ancient times when royals would forbid commoners to be festive in case their celebrations lead to uprisings. Others believe the Industrial Revolution cultivated a belief that work and productivity held more importance than frivolity (to keep us on track!). However, like with other emotions, if children are taught to suppress joy, they are at risk of developing problematic patterns of relating to others and the world. In other words, we need to strive for a "happy" medium where joy is cultivated to create resilience, just like other emotions.

Reflections

What might make it hard for me to put into words my child's experience in a situation like this?

_____

_____

_____

What might make it hard for me to get practical in a situation like this?

_____

_____

_____

What do I need to deal with a situation like this more confidently in the future?

_____

_____

_____

"My Tummy Hurts ..." 9

We've started this chapter with a physical complaint because it's really common for children (and all people, in fact) to feel their feelings in their body. Sometimes a spade is just a spade and it's purely physical, and so you don't want to start by assuming all pain or bodily symptoms are caused by emotions. Young kids often get stomachaches with viruses, for example. However, if your child repeatedly complains of physical symptoms, especially right before school, bedtime, or high stress events, you may consider that some anxiety or other strong emotion may be contributing to the symptoms. The mind and body are intricately connected so that feeling unwell physically can cause emotional stress and emotional stress can cause physical symptoms. It's not an either–or situation but a "both–and." Just think of how you get "butterflies in your stomach" before public speaking or your cheeks flush red when angry or embarrassed. For the purpose of this chapter, let's assume your health care provider has confirmed there is no purely physical cause to explain the degree of your child's symptoms, and there is at least some part better explained by the expression of emotion through physical feelings and complaints.

Scenario: "My Tummy Hurts ..."

In this scenario, it's a Monday morning before school and your child says, for the fourth time this month: "My tummy really hurts."

The Knee-Jerk Response

Much of the time, parents and caregivers will respond with something like:

"You probably just have to go to the bathroom."

"Where does it hurt? Do you need a tummy massage"

Sometimes, especially when frustrated, one might say:

"Right. Just like last night when it was time to clean up, you suddenly have a tummy ache."

Imagine for a moment that your child says to you his version of "My tummy hurts ..."

What's your most likely knee-jerk response?

_____

_____

_____

 # Step 1. Building a Bridge

Kids who complain of pain most often do feel pain, whether or not it's triggered or increased by anxiety. Pain is complex, and even the discomfort associated with well-known medical illnesses is often worsened by stress for example. It's really not "all in their head"; the pain kids feel with stress can be just as real as the pain of a skinned knee. Children who feel tense in the morning before school are likely anticipating being uncomfortable. It may only be their body reacting, or there may be thoughts about the anticipated stress. Kids of all ages, from toddler to young adult, can have physical symptoms of anxiety that affect their seeming willingness to go to school. Kids may fear having to do something they struggle with in class, having to interact with adults they don't know well, peer rejection and embarrassment, or just being away from home. They may be highly motivated to get to school or their activity, but the anxiety and related physical symptoms are so strong that they make it look like the child is unwilling, stubborn, or not motivated.

Possible Emotion Translations

Possibility A: "I'm worried I'll feel overwhelmed with missing you!"
Possibility B: "I'm scared Mrs. Ambrose will be upset with me."

Possibility C: "My best friend was away all last week and I'm stressed that I'll have no one to play with at recess again. It's so uncomfortable when that happens!"

Translations for your child:

_____

_____

_____

💬 Step 2. Putting It into Words

Option 1. "Oh, dear. It's that tummy again. It's really bugging you. I wonder if it's a 'missing-hurt.' It seems to hurt when you're worried you'll miss Mommy. It would make sense if it did."

Option 2. "That pain is telling us something really important. I wonder if it's telling us that you're worried about Mrs. Ambrose or about what could happen at recess if Paige is away from school again today."

Option 3. "I can see from your face that it really hurts. And maybe you worry that when you get to school it will get even worse and you won't be able to manage."

In your own words:

I can imagine why you would have a sore tummy because _____, and because _____, and because _____.

*Reminder: This is another scenario where we don't stop here. While acknowledging the child's feelings and experience may help her feel to better, she is likely to need our emotional and practical support to move forward.

Step 3. Getting Practical

Emotional support: Kids who frequently complain of physical symptoms often have a harder time noticing, recognizing and talking about their feelings. They may also hesitate to ask directly for emotional comfort. Parents can help by offering a hug, a cuddle, or soothing and reassuring words. For example, "Sounds like you need a big hug from Mommy. I am never far away, and I believe in you so much." Parents can also show kids through their words and their presence that it's ok to show "negative" emotions ("I might even feel like crying if that happened to me. It would be totally normal to feel sad"). When you target the emotions, because they naturally rise and pass, your child is more likely to feel better faster, even if butterflies remain.

Practical support: Assuming the child is anxious because of a situation like those above, it's important to support her in facing her fear. Protecting her from a situation is helpful for a real danger, but not as a response to anxiety or physical discomfort. The more children avoid something, the more anxious and avoidant they become. When children get anxious or feel unwell, they almost always need their caregivers to use kind firmness to help them get through it. Parents can show confidence in the child and determination about getting the child where they need to be. The key here is for parents to take the lead in moving forward, rather than waiting for the child to be "ready." Anxiety and physical discomfort can be very persuasive, but they shouldn't take over the family. Here are some examples of ways to communicate this:

> Lots of kids miss their mommies at preschool. Let's pack a stuffy with you today and I'll give the stuffy a big hug. If you miss me, you can hug the stuffy, and I will see you right after dress-up time.

> As much as your tummy hurts right now, I know that it usually gets better once you're outside and on the walk to school. We can figure out a way for you to deal with Mrs. Ambrose while we walk, and if you need me to help to speak with her, I will.

Although a list of behavioral strategies for anxiety is beyond the scope of this book, here are a few basic ideas:

During the episode:

1. Help the child focus on something they like that will come during or after the activity (e.g. "don't forget you get to see Marnie after school today").
2. Change scenery (e.g. "let's go outside and check out the pond").
3. Mentally break the task into smaller, more manageable steps, and start with the first step. (e.g. "let's focus on getting dressed for right now and then we'll see how you're doing").
4. Offer two choices for how to proceed (e.g. "you can get your backpack or water bottle and I'll get the other").

5.   Set clear expectations and time limits (e.g. "Time to get dressed. I'll set the timer for 5 minutes").

Before next time:

1.   Practice mindfulness and relaxation strategies like noticing body sensations and belly breathing (it really does work!).
2.   Have a good routine in place and ensure you have enough time around the tough spot.
3.   Sit down with your child and list the parts of the task, easiest to hardest. This is often done by drawing a "challenge ladder" or thermometer. When everyone is calm, practice the easier parts before moving one by one to the more challenging ones. This is called "gradual exposure."

You can check out Chapter 24: Recommended Readings for resources to help kids with anxiety, avoidance and stress-sensitive physical symptoms.

Sample Script: "My Tummy Hurts …"

CHILD: "My tummy hurts."
PARENT: "Oh, dear. It's that tummy again. It's really bugging you."
CHILD: "It just really hurts, Mommy. I can't go to school today."
PARENT: "I wonder if it's a 'missing-hurt' or a 'worried-about-what-might-happen-today-hurt'."
CHILD: "I just don't want to go."
PARENT: "I can see from your face that it's really painful. And maybe you're worried that when you get to school, it will get even worse. Or maybe that you won't be able to manage."
CHILD: "Yeah, Mr. Jones won't listen if I tell him it hurts."
PARENT: "I wonder if there's a way you can feel a little better about telling Mr. Jones if you need to. Do you have any ideas?"
CHILD: "Can you write him an email?"
PARENT: "I can do that. And I'll tell him that usually when your tummy hurts, a little walk and some water can help a lot. Does that sound good?"
CHILD: "Okay, but when are you going to be home from work?"
PARENT: "I'll be there to pick you up from after-school care. I wonder if you're a little worried about missing me."
CHILD: (tears up a bit) "Can we play a game after school?"

PARENT: "Absolutely, sweetheart. It's a long day, and I'll be thinking about you too, and we'll be sure to snuggle and play after school."

CHILD: (starting to get out from under covers) "Okay. I'm going to put on my blue shirt today."

Common Pitfalls

1. "What's the big deal if she takes a 'mental health day'"? The occasional day off for a child isn't the end of the world, BUT once children figure out that it's possible or acceptable to stay home from school, it becomes much more likely they will expect to again in the future. It is worth the effort to get young kids to school when they're anxious or a little unwell because it teaches the child and family how to cope with the child's distress. This is a tough issue, and it may require the support of a mental health or other health professional, but it's worth getting to the bottom of school resistance when kids are young to get the tools they need. It is not a pattern that kids easily grow out of without support.

2. "He's just faking it!" The line between "faking" and stress-sensitive pain is a hard one to figure out. Actual "faking" means purposely deceiving an adult to get something you want (or avoid something you don't want). Kids absolutely do "fake" illness and injury to get out of chores, school, and other stuff they don't want to do, but you need to ask yourself why they are doing it. Based on one of our guiding principles that "kids will be good if they can be," we can assume that a kid who is "faking" is still communicating a problem. It is still likely to be stress about something they want to avoid. It may be anger at you or someone else or just not enough 1:1 time. Either way, you won't lose anything by validating their behavior. If you call the child's bluff directly and he snaps into action, then great. That may work well when the child doesn't want to do something (e.g., clean his room) but when the avoidance is based on anxiety (e.g., fear of public speaking at school), insinuating the child is "faking" or saying it's "all in his head" will usually only lead them to dig in further and become even more avoidant or defiant.

3. "She'll be fine. She needs to just suck it up." Many parents will tell us that their own parents would have never stood for this kind of thing and just sent them to school no matter what. There are benefits to a harder line, and it can be effective for some kids. However, there are kids for whom the "pull yourself up by the bootstraps" approach doesn't work as well. These are usually kids who are "super-feelers," in that they experience emotions in a bigger way – their own and those of others, and/or who have more significant anxiety, mental or physical health issues, or who have already been in a pattern of avoiding school for a while. In these instances, emotional support is key. There may also be a danger (physical or emotional) that your child is avoiding. If the child's stress or anxiety is related to mistreatment or bullying, getting practical is essential. No amount of comfort, reassurance, or encouragement will be enough to help a child feel comfortable going to school when he is faced with bullies or mistreatment by an adult. The first steps may include talking to your child about his experience and encouraging him to stay nearby other helpful students and adults. The action plan may also need to include speaking to the teacher or principal to escalate the attention to the problem. With peer conflict, it's fine to teach kids how to be more assertive; for true bullying (a persistent pattern of unwelcome or aggressive behavior that involves an imbalance of power or the intention to harm or humiliate someone), adults do need to become involved. We've included additional resources at the end of the book for this situation should it be the case for your child.

What might make it hard for me to put into words my child's experience in a situation like this?

_____

_____

_____

What might make it hard for me to get practical in this situation?

_____

_____

_____

What do I need to deal with this situation more confidently in the future is?

_____

_____

_____

Figure 9.1 The knee-jerk response

Figure 9.2 Validation and support

"I'm Not Talking to You ..." **10**

Some of you may be reading this book and feeling like this approach won't work because "my child just won't talk to me about certain things." How can you connect emotionally with a child who isn't even giving you fodder to translate? Thankfully, we can use the same framework with silence and we've found it to be more likely to open up those lines of communication than using more forceful language such as "That's not nice – I'm talking to you," or, on the other end of the spectrum, – leaving the ball entirely in their court, since it may take forever for them to volley back.

Scenario: "I'm Not Talking to You ..."

The Knee-Jerk Response

Much of the time, parents and caregivers will respond with something like:

"Honey, don't be rude. I asked you a question."

"How I can help you if you won't even tell me what's wrong?"

Sometimes, especially when frustrated, one might say:

"Fine, but don't say I didn't try!"

Imagine for a moment that your child says to you her version of "I'm not talking to you ..."

What's your most likely knee-jerk response?

_____

_____

_____

Step 1. Building a Bridge

When a child is silent or refuses to engage, the disconnection can be painful for all involved, especially if you interpret their behavior as disrespectful or rejecting. The first thing to remember is that children have much less verbal capacity than adults. Even ones who make really cute and precocious comments don't necessarily understand all our words. Some school-age kids (and some adults!) still find talking about feelings really hard. Play is the easiest and most natural language for kids. Drawing and other art forms may come next. So when a child says he doesn't want to talk to you, he may simply be saying, "Talking about ___(specified topic)___ is too hard for me right now." If this is the case for your child, you may find playing with them, drawing together or even writing to each other much more successful. It's amazing that children will inevitably "bring up the topic" that needs to be discussed in drawing or play if given enough time in your presence to do so (usually 20 minutes is enough).

If, on the other hand, you have a child who normally talks, and this is a clear signal that something's up, read on. Although your child may come across as "wanting space," be assured that there are strong (and often vulnerable) underlying emotions that need attention. Often, a child is angry with the parent but worried that the expression of anger will lead to trouble. On the other hand, some children resist revealing what's going on for them if they worry about their parent's capacity to handle what they have to share. They don't want to overwhelm or hurt their parent. They also don't want to be met with attempts to correct their experience or solve the problem. You know your child best, so it will be important for you to connect with that wisdom to sort out which of the scenarios is most likely at play.

Possible Emotion Translations

Possibility A: "I'm really mad at you, and the only way I can show you just how upset I am is to shut you out."

Possibility B: "I want to talk to you, but I'm scared you'll be upset with me or you'll tell me to change the way I'm feeling or push me to find a solution."

Possibility C: "I'm overwhelmed and wish I could make this problem disappear. When you talk to me about it, it brings it to the surface and I get even more overwhelmed."

Translations for your child:

_____

_____

_____

⟨💬⟩ Step 2. Putting It into Words

Option 1. "I don't blame you for not wanting to talk to me. Sometimes I rush to fix or try to convince you to feel a different way. It might feel like there's no point."

Option 2. "I can see you need some space. That makes sense because what I did really upset you. You didn't think how I handled it was fair."

Option 3. "I know that sometimes when we talk about things it can feel even worse. I can imagine that not talking about it gives you a break from the feelings."

In your own words:

I can imagine why you'd not want to talk to me because _____, and because _____, and because _____.

*Reminder: First, try to guess the context: Did something just happen recently? Does your child have a pattern of getting upset in similar situations? They key is to ask yourself: What is the most vulnerable explanation for my child's silence?

Step 3. Getting Practical

Emotional support: If children don't want to talk because they feel hurt, sad, or anxious, then saying they don't want to talk is more often a way to protect themselves from feeling vulnerable. Overwhelmed children also need your calm presence, but with less pressure to resolve anything quickly or verbalize emotions. They need things to go slowly and to face problems in small bits at a time. That may mean that sitting with you quietly fidgeting or playing with something is all they can tolerate at first.

If you suspect the silence reflects feelings of anger, the emotional need for this one is a little counterintuitive. On the one hand, the angry child is clearly saying "I need space"; on the other hand, no child ever really wants to be left totally alone. If she's mad at you, then being left alone for a bit makes sense so she can cool down, while knowing you are around and will return in a specified amount of time to keep working through the disconnection. It can also be important to consider that the distance each kid needs may be different. For some, distance means in the same room but without a ton of talking or connection. For others, staying just outside the door of the bedroom or bathroom or even all the way across the room is as close as they can tolerate in the short term.

If it makes sense to do so, you may even consider offering an apology to let your child know you're invested in his feelings and you recognize that whatever pattern you were in together didn't unfold as you would have wanted. Apologies can be incredibly powerful, so long as they come from a place of calm, compassion, and confidence – in other words, you're neither self-flagellating ("It's all my fault; I keep messing up") nor "wordsmithing" to get out of actually taking a share of the responsibility ("I'm sorry you feel that way"). An effective apology communicates remorse and responsibility ("I'm sorry my actions hurt you") and leaves out explanations, justifications or blame.

Practical support: My wise coworker said that if she ever wrote a book on parenting, it would be called *Mothers Not Allowed; Daughters Always Welcome*. She was referring to the fact that even if her daughter shut her out and didn't talk about things, as a mother, she would always be open to when her daughter wanted to talk. She recognized that it's not meant to be an equal relationship and that when children are hurt and try to push parents away, they still need to know we can't ever fully be pushed away. At the same time, to allow us to be close, kids need a way to assert their boundaries. It's almost impossible to teach this while the child is angry, shutdown, or refusing to talk, so once things are calm again, you can figure out a way to let your child know that he's allowed to have some space and that you aren't too fragile to be told what's bothering him, even if it's about you. It has to be genuine, of course, because despite what you say, if you react strongly to whatever she tells you, she is likely to clam up again. If your child has been withdrawn, shutdown, or refusing to talk to you for weeks or months, then it may take a third-party or professional to help open the lines of communication. If that's the case, don't despair, we help parents and kids reconnect all the time, and it can be fairly straightforward.

Sample Script: "I'm Not Talking to You …"

PARENT: "Hey, hon. How was your visit with Mom?"

CHILD: (clearly fighting back emotion) "Fine."

PARENT: "What's up? What happened?"

CHILD: "Nothing. And I don't want to talk about it."

PARENT: "I see. Well if something happened, I can't help you unless you tell me."

CHILD: "It's fine, Dad."

PARENT: "Ah, I think I know what's going on. When I put myself in your position, I wouldn't want to tell me either. For many reasons."

CHILD: (silence)

PARENT: "Well for starters you're a kid who appreciates privacy, and I know that talking about your feelings is not your favorite thing to do."

CHILD: (silence)

PARENT: "And we've been butting heads a lot lately, so you might expect more of that. Like I might lecture you or tell you not to feel the way you do."

CHILD: (silence)

PARENT: "And if something happened with Mom or you two got in a fight, I imagine you would be hesitant to tell me in case I got mad at her too. As much as you might want to vent, you probably don't want me to jump on the bandwagon – especially since you know that she and I sometimes don't get along so well."

CHILD: (nodding)

PARENT: "Before we got divorced, I was a lot better at listening to your feelings *and* helping you to see her side too. As much as you didn't like it that I sometimes 'defended' her, I bet that it felt better than when I just join you in your frustration."

CHILD: "Or that you'll send her another one of your emails and then make it awkward for me next week! I love Mom – even when

I'm mad at her – and I need that to be okay! And if it is okay – then I can tell you when she does something to make me feel sad or mad without worrying what you'll think of her or what you'll do to try to fix it. I just want it to be normal."

PARENT: "Of course you do, my love. And no wonder you didn't want to talk to me about whatever happened. It makes total sense to me."

CHILD: (silence)

PARENT: "And the truth is, even though your Mom and I are in a rough patch – we're going to figure this out in a good way, and I am going to do my part to remember what I need to do – support you and think the best of mom. Okay – let's try this again … What happened this weekend, sweetie?"

CHILD: "Fine – I'll tell you, but please don't make it a thing!"

PARENT: "I'll tell you what – as long as your safety isn't at risk – I promise not to make it a thing."

CHILD: "Dad. My safety is *not* at risk. Geez!"

PARENT: "Okay then – we've got a deal!"

Common Pitfalls

1. "But what if she's hiding something terrible?" When your child refuses to speak to you it can be really unnerving – even scary – especially if your imagination leads you to believe that something really bad happened. This can lead one to respond with a high degree of stress: "You *have* to tell me what's going on!" The child who is already shut down and overwhelmed will likely get even more closed off and resistant when he feels the intensity of the stress. Your best tool here is calm, patience and – you guessed it – validation using a few because-statements to put their thoughts or feelings into words.

2. "I would *never* have dared give my parents the silent treatment." If you interpret the silence as disrespectful, you might react with anger. It's true – shutting someone out isn't necessarily respectful, especially in some cultures. The problem is, even if you demand respect or implement consequences for refusing to talk, children may only tell you what they think you want to hear or what is most likely to minimize the chance of punishment. We would never suggest that you should allow insults or language that crosses your line, but being curious about why your child is refusing to talk tends to yield more in the long run than reacting with anger or consequences. In our experience, when parents get angry at a kid's refusal to talk, this adds more fuel to the fire within the child who is already weighted down by some other emotional issue.

3. "I'm devastated. He should be able to talk to me about anything." Some parents forget about how strong the neurobiological bond between parent and child really is, and that a small bump in communication or even a brief total breakdown isn't going to cause lasting damage. This comes up a lot in split-family situations or when your child goes through the different phases of preferring one parent's company to another. It also starts to come up more in the preteen years as your child starts developing normal needs for independence. It can feel like his temporary refusal to talk to you is a reflection of your overall relationship ("He doesn't love me as much as he used to"/"He doesn't trust me") or your parenting abilities ("See, I'm getting it all wrong; otherwise why would he refuse to talk to me?"). If you think you may have done something that the child is angry about, you can always apologize, as described above; however, sometimes the child's refusal to talk isn't about the parent or the quality of the parent–child relationship at all. It really can be all about the child feeling too overwhelmed to be able to put thoughts into words. If you notice lots of self-blame in your mind or a strong feeling of rejection when you child shuts you out, that may push you to want to reconcile with your child ASAP so you can feel better. This is totally normal but needs to be balanced with your child's need for time; otherwise, he's likely to feel pressure to "make up" with you before the feelings have run their course.

Reflections

What might make it hard for me to put into words my child's experience in a situation like this?

_____

_____

_____

What might make it hard for me to get practical in a situation like this?

_____

_____

_____

What do I need to deal with a situation like this more confidently in the future?

_____

_____

_____

"I'm so Bad/Stupid ..." **11**

We all have moments when we're not proud of something we've done. A rare statement from your child like "I'm such an idiot" isn't usually a cause for concern. However, some children get into a pattern of putting themselves down or have major episodes of self-criticism. When a child engages in harsh self-criticism, once she is calm, you can help her see all the great things about her, but in the heat of the moment, reassurance is unlikely to have the desired effect. Self-blame can also be a way to deal with negative feelings. It can feel better for children to blame themselves than to get blamed – at least there's more control in it. Regardless of the fuel for the self-blame, our task is to help our children find a better way to express their negative feelings.

Scenario A: "I'm so Bad ..."

Let's say your child breaks one of his parents' belongings or gets in trouble for something he's done wrong. It can be right away or later on that they say some version of "I'm a bad kid."

The Knee-Jerk Response

Much of the time, parents and caregivers will respond with something like:

"No, you're not! You're a good boy/girl."

"Honey, you shouldn't think that; it was your behavior that was bad."

Sometimes, especially when frustrated, one might say:

"Yes, you were bad. You need to do better next time."

Imagine a scenario where your child says to you his version of "I'm so bad ..."

What's your most likely knee-jerk response?

_____

_____

_____

 ## Step 1. Building a Bridge

At their core, kids want to be accepted by their parents. When they've behaved badly, they often worry they will be rejected or that their parents won't love them anymore. Children who insult themselves are usually feeling shame. They can't separate out the fact that a negative behavior doesn't make someone a bad person. Especially when children are repeatedly struggling with their behavior, they may feel like they are doomed to continue losing control and hurting others or getting in trouble. Sometimes they fear punishment and would rather criticize themselves as a shield from a parent's criticism or to show that they are remorseful. Other times, their self-criticism is an expression of feelings like guilt, anxiety or anger that they just don't know how to communicate in a more appropriate or direct way. They don't yet understand that almost any situation can be worked through with some support.

Possible Emotion Translations

Possibility A: "I'm worried that I'll never stop misbehaving/hurting others/getting in trouble."

Possibility B: "I'm ashamed at how I just behaved and I want to show you badly I feel about it so that you won't be as mad at me or love me less."

Possibility C: "I'm so upset about the mistake I made that I can't stand it."

Translations for your child:

_____

_____

_____

 **Step 2. Putting It into Words**

Option 1. "Oh, honey. I see that you feel badly about yourself, maybe because you worry this will keep happening or that there must be something wrong with you to keep getting in trouble."

Option 2. "You're *really* regretting what you did."

Option 3. "Sounds like you're worried I'll think less of you for this. You want to make sure we're okay."

In your own words:

I can imagine why you would feel "bad" because _____, and because _____, and because _____.

As in other chapters, it may feel pretty icky to make these kinds of statements in case it conveys agreement, especially with something so hurtful for the child. Remember that validation isn't agreement. This is the first step in helping your child feel understood so that he can be open to what's coming up next – your support.

 Step 3. Getting Practical

Emotional support: In response to shame and anxiety about being "bad" or defective in some way, children do need to know that you see their goodness and that their actions don't define them. Providing validation first will open the door for this kind of support to make its way into their inner world.

For example:
"I might be angry, but I will always love you no matter what."

or

"All people, even adults, make mistakes and break things/hurt people."

We want our children to learn self-compassion: to be loving and accepting toward themselves. The easiest way to learn this is by experiencing compassion from caregivers. When children feel good about themselves, they're also way more likely to "do good" too. It's a simple equation that's pretty predictable, although hard to remember when things get really tense, especially when you want them to learn a lesson.

Practical support: When a child does something hurtful or harmful, most often, the practical need is to make amends. Even young children can participate in a process of reconciliation. Doing so teaches our children that it's possible to repair ruptures and strengthen relationships; that most often there is a solution. For a young child, making amends may be helping to repair something broken or with the clean-up. Older children can be involved in all aspects of this process. I once worked with a child who broke the classroom computer. He felt extremely ashamed. His teachers worked with him on a plan to make amends that included volunteering for duties around the school to earn some of the money to pay for the computer. When I saw him weeks later, he felt extremely proud of his contribution. No written or verbal apology could have affected his sense of self like the practical work he did to improve the situation.

Sample Script: "I'm so Bad …"

Your child is banging his truck on the pavement, and a wheel falls off. He starts to sob.

CHILD: "No! I broke my truck! I am a bad boy! I am a very bad boy!"

PARENT: "Oh dear, let me see what happened. I bet you feel really bad about that."

CHILD: (nodding in agreement)

PARENT: "I wonder if you're also a little scared that you're going to get in trouble for breaking your toy."

CHILD: (nodding in agreement)

PARENT: Maybe when you say that you're a bad boy, it's a way to show Mommy that you feel bad that you were banging your toy and that you're scared about what I will say."

CHILD: (nodding in agreement)

PARENT: "Looks like that broken truck taught you a hard lesson about being more gentle. Now that you've learned the lesson, it will be easier to remember the next time. Making mistakes doesn't make you a bad boy, though. It really doesn't. It wasn't a good choice, but you've learned from it, and now we can figure out what to do next."

CHILD: "What do you mean?"

PARENT: "Well, we can pretend the truck needs to go to the garage for repairs and see if glue will work to get that wheel back on. Or we can say thank you to the toy for the fun and see about recycling it."

CHILD: "If the wheel is stuck on with glue, it won't turn. (sigh) I guess we can recycle it."

*Reminder: Your ace in the hole is sincerity. Thanks to their mirror neurons, your child's brain will register that your efforts are genuine, leading to a release of calming neurochemicals regardless of how well you follow the structure provided.

Common Pitfalls

1. "Wait – isn't feeling bad about bad behavior a good thing?" Yes, the experience of guilt after we've done something hurtful or harmful is actually an adaptive response. Healthy guilt is a built-in signaling system letting us know that we've gone against our values or the values of the group with which we belong (like our family, our class or our peer group). In other words, guilt helps us to learn how to navigate future challenges in a way that is respectful to ourselves and others. However, when children feel *shame*, it can be corrosive to their sense of self. Among other possibilities, they are more likely to withdraw or act out – including with aggression. As Brené Brown made clear in her TED talk "Listening to Shame," guilt is related to a behavior, whereas shame is a focus on self. In other words, guilt is, "I did something bad" (and I need to learn from it), whereas shame is, "I am bad" (and I am unworthy).

2. "That sounds like my inner critic! What have I done to my child?" If a parent has struggled with a harsh inner critic, hearing a child criticize herself in this way can trigger self-blame (it's my fault that she thinks so negatively about herself) or worry that the child will develop low self-esteem or depression. It can feel paralyzing – sometimes to the point that it's hard to focus on what's going on for the child, including what to say and do. See Chapter 4: Staying on Track for ways to manage the worry and self-blame that may come up so that you can regain access to your instincts and what you've learned.

Reflections

What might make it hard for me to put into words my child's experience in a situation like this?

_____

_____

_____

What might make it hard for me to get practical in a situation like this?

_____

_____

_____

What do I need to deal with a situation like this more confidently in the future?

_____

_____

_____

Scenario B: "I'm so Stupid ..."

In this situation, imagine an older child impulsively tells a friend a secret she was supposed to keep for another girl. When the girl finds out, she disinvites your daughter from her birthday party. She's now at home, crying in her bedroom. When you come in to check up on her, she responds with "Leave me alone! I am so stupid!"

The Knee-Jerk Response

Much of the time, parents and caregivers will respond with something like:

"Why don't you try calling her? Or I can call and talk to her mother?"

"Everyone makes mistakes. There will be other birthday parties."

Sometimes, especially when frustrated, one might say:

"Yeah, that was a bad move. I hope you learned your lesson!"

Imagine for a moment that your child says to you her version of "I'm so stupid …"

What's your most likely knee-jerk response?

_____

_____

_____

 ## Step 1. Building a Bridge

With older kids, the mishaps are often a bit more complicated. It may be losing at a game, getting rejected by a crush or not knowing something their older sibling does. When children call themselves "stupid" or some other insult, they are usually struggling to deal with the bad feeling that comes from making a mistake, whether that evaluation is objective or through the eyes of the child.

Possible Emotion Translations

Possibility A: "I should have been able to do better. Messing up like this makes me question how good I am."

Possibility B: "I'm so embarrassed by what happened, and mad at myself for not knowing better. I wish I could go back in time and act differently."

Possibility C: "I'm worried that no one will forgive my mistake. I'm scared I'll be excluded from the group forever."

Translations for your child:

_____

_____

_____

Step 2. Putting It into Words

Option 1. "No wonder you feel bad for telling the secret. You never meant for it to go this far and you think you should have known better."

Option 2. "You can't let yourself off the hook for this one. I think I get it. Maybe you're worried that she won't forgive you and you feel like it's all your fault."

Option 3. "I can see why you're upset. You really care about her and you want things to be okay between you."

In your own words:

I can imagine why you would feel stupid because _____, and be-cause _____, and because _____.

*Reminder: Although these statements are meant to calm the storm in the brain, we don't want to stop there. If we did, it could feel like a bit of a cliffhanger. It's once you've spoken their perspective that your child will be more open to your emotional and practical support.

Step 3. Getting Practical

Emotional support: Self-criticism and obsessively thinking about mis-takes are ways the brain tries to cope with big feelings that feel bad. In Chapter 4, we talked about self-compassion for parents; this is a situation where we can help kids develop perspective and self-compassion. It's possible that your child hasn't yet examined all the factors and is unre-alistically putting all the blame on herself. You can help her see her own actions as a smaller part of the whole. You can remind your child that everyone does something they wish they hadn't from time to time; it's part of being human. In this situation, your child will likely to be able to work it out with her peer group, so you can give her some realistic hope around this. You can also remind your child that just like criticizing others isn't a great strategy to motivate people to do better (would they want their coach or teacher to speak to them in this way?), when we criticize ourselves, we end up intensifying the weight of the stress and feeling even less capable of finding a way forward.

If the situation can't be easily remedied, then you can still help your child think kind and compassionate thoughts for herself and the per-son or people she feels she may have hurt or wronged. There are many books and apps for teaching mindfulness and self-compassion to kids (see Chapter 24: Recommended Readings). Being with her and helping her sit with her tough feelings is a huge amount of emotional support and demonstrates the compassion you hope she will one day learn to show herself.

Practical need. Once you've provided some orientation to the big picture, the practical strategy that will help the most involves getting back on the horse – in other words, to face people again. Peer relationships and acceptance are extremely important to older kids. Your role can be to help your child make amends by brainstorming and problem-solving with her how to approach the situation and then helping her practice what to say to the person she feels she's wronged. For example:

"As bad as this feels, I'm pretty sure that your friend will forgive you. Let's sit down together and think of some ways to reach out to her?"

or

"Absolutely everyone messes up in friendships. (Insert your own embarrassing story.) Let's think of some options for dealing with the situation now."

When kids are stuck on replay for big feelings or self-criticism and we've gone through the framework once or twice, sometimes the most helpful thing we can do is to get them off their current brain-track. A short-term distraction can get the child "unstuck." Suggest something active like going for a walk, something connecting like playing a game of cards, or something easy and enjoyable like listening to music. Once your child has settled a bit, she may then be more able to try the other ideas above.

Note: If your child is feeling "stupid" about academic achievement, then there may or may not be a need to redo a test or assignment or to help the child have more realistic expectations for her performance. In these cases, refer to Chapter 15: "I Got a Terrible Mark …" for more tips to navigate these types of interactions.

Sample Script: "I'm so Stupid …"

Imagine that 12-year-old Sonia has forwarded a social media survey to a boy she likes. It has options to check mark questions like: "Do you like me?"; "Are we friends?"; "Do you want to meet at recess?" He checks the box for "no" for every single one. She runs down from her room crying.

CHILD: "I'm so stupid! I should have never sent it!"
PARENT: "Sent what?"
CHILD: "Never mind, you'll never understand!"
PARENT: "No wait, come here. You sound furious at yourself for something that obviously didn't go well."
CHILD: "Yeah, well I'm a total idiot! Anyone else would have known better. Kayden basically told me he hates me."
PARENT: "Oh that's terrible. What happened?"
CHILD: The child recounts the incident.
PARENT: "Aw, and now you can't let yourself off the hook for this because it seems like everyone else would have seen this coming."
CHILD: "They would have! Sydney told me he didn't like me, and I still wanted to find out for myself."
PARENT: "Of course you're upset – it hurts so much when someone says they don't like you back. Even worse when it's right in front of your face."
CHILD: (crying now) "I really liked him."
PARENT: "Oh honey, I'm so sorry you're hurting. Can I give you a hug?"
CHILD: (comes closer) "Okay."

*Reminder: The proposed framework is not a magic formula. It can also feel really awkward because it goes against so much of what we were taught about how to respond to children's thoughts and feelings. We do urge you to try it out a few times following the steps as closely as possible as practice really does make a difference over time.

Common Pitfalls

1. "If I say: 'I can understand why you'd call yourself stupid ... ', won't I give him the message that he is?" Sounding like you agree with the child's criticism of himself is a common concern among parents, and that's exactly the opposite of what you want to do! There is no need to repeat the exact name the child calls himself, just to put the underlying feelings into more descriptive words. Also, if you put into words your child's feelings or perceptions of himself without then offering the emotional and practical support – then yes, you run the risk that the child misunderstands your intentions. However, when the because-statements are then followed by the support strategies, in particular reassurance and big-picture orientation, what we have found is that doing so doesn't actually make the child think the parent agrees. Instead it helps the child feel less badly about himself because he feels loved and understood even in his dark place. Once you join him there, your offers to help will actually have the desired effect, although you may need to offer a couple of rounds of because-statements and emotional support depending on the severity of the issue.

2. "She should have known better. Now she has to face the consequences." When your child behaves really badly, especially if she hurts someone else, it can feel like the most important thing to do is to draw the child's attention to her mistake and correct the misbehavior. This is important, but some children need us to attend to their feelings of hurt, shame, remorse, or anger *before* they can learn anything new about how to treat others better. If their emotions are high, their capacity to learn or engage in problem-solving is equally low. Attending to your child's distress by putting it into words will help calm her brain to help her to get to a place of being able to have more empathy for the other person.

Reflections

What might make it hard for me to put into words my child's experience in a situation like this?

_____

_____

_____

What might make it hard for me to get practical in a situation like this?

_____

_____

_____

What do I need to deal with a situation like this more confidently in the future?

_____

_____

_____

"You Just Don't Get It!" 12

When our kids are infants, we constantly have to guess what they need, and even then, it's trial and error. The older and more complex their thoughts, feelings, and lives become, the more often we struggle to know exactly what's going on. The truth is that children may also understand some aspects of culture, especially youth and school culture, that we simply do not. Preteens may start holding back more in their attempt to be independent. Part of this normal development may also include rejecting some of what parents think and believe. Yet when children yell "You just don't get it," they usually mean more specifically that we aren't getting something important about their feelings, thoughts or experience.

Scenario A: "You Just Don't Get It!"

Your rules about screen time are clear: no screens before homework on weekdays. You find your child on his device right after school and ask him to take a break. He powers off and angrily yells, "You just don't get it!"

The Knee-Jerk Response

Much of the time, parents and caregivers will respond with something like:

"Honey, the rules are for your sake. That much screen time isn't good for you."

"I was a kid too. I didn't like when my parents told me what to do, but I didn't talk back."

Sometimes, especially when frustrated, one might say:

(sarcastically) "You're right, when I was a kid we played a game called 'outside.'"

Imagine for a moment that your child says to you his version of "You just don't get it!"

What's your most likely knee-jerk response?

_____

_____

_____

 ## Step 1. Building a Bridge

The hidden gem in "you just don't get it" is a genuine wish to be understood, and by you. It sounds like a criticism (and really not the best way for them to go about it), yet it's actually an invitation to keep trying. It also implies that the child likely hasn't felt understood on this topic or other topics in the past. You may understand her extremely well most of the time and in hundreds of ways, but it's all about the child's *perception* in that moment. What's it like to not feel understood? Frustrating. It can make you feel angry or disappointed or even hurt or alone. These are the possible feelings under the criticism.

Possible Emotion Translations

Possibility A: "I feel alone with this, and I really want you to join me where I'm at."

Possibility B: "This topic is a really hard one for me. When you don't get it exactly right on the first try, it hurts and I worry it won't go well."

Possibility C: "I want you to know that my feelings are so big and complicated right now that it seems like no one could ever possibly understand them."

Translations for your child:

_____

_____

_____

Step 2. Putting It into Words

Option 1. "It might feel like every time you want to play, I tell you to shut it off. It might be like I don't get how important the game is to you."

Option 2. "I guess it feels impossible to get through to me because you keep trying to explain, and I keep setting the rules. I don't blame you for feeling frustrated."

Option 3: "You're absolutely right. There is no way for me to fully understand what it's like for you and that's really tough."

In your own words:

I can imagine why you'd feel like I won't ever get it because _____, and because _____, and because _____.

Step 3. Getting Practical

Emotional support: "You just don't get it" is an invitation for conversation and connection. You may communicate to them that you are willing to try again. If they are still angry or shut down, it may mean that there's been a history of feeling alone or misunderstood that needs to be addressed; we cover this in more detail in Chapter 19: The "Do-Over."

The relationship may also benefit from an apology such as:

> I know that I wasn't able to understand the last time we tried to talk about this. I get that it would seem like there's no point trying

again because it didn't go well before and I've been quick to set the limit. I'm really sorry for (being distracted/not giving you air time/not finding a way to get to the bottom of it) and I'd like to try again.

There is always another chance, as long as we're sincere in our wish to understand. You may not be able to have the conversation right then and there, but you can always set a time to discuss it further a little later.

"Zoe, I can see this is really important to you. I have to go out this evening, but how about we talk it over during dinner tomorrow?"

Practical support: In this scenario and others like it, the practical need can involve teaching direct and assertive communication. Parents are encouraged to take the lead on the conversation and encourage kids to explain themselves. It really helps here to convey genuine curiosity and a sincere desire to understand their perspective. It's also important to assume that the child has a positive intention. In this scenario, the positive intention is the desire to socialize with friends online. On the other hand, kids don't always spontaneously have the ability to understand their parent's perspective. To this child, it may be obvious that a video game isn't all bad: It's fun *and* it's social. He doesn't know that his parents didn't have online games growing up. So our job is to figure out where the child is coming from and help him do the same with us.

Usually, once there is a deeper level of mutual understanding, a reasonable negotiation follows. Even if nothing changes in the practical limits you set, your child will feel better understood and build confidence by learning to state his point of view.

*Reminder: Your ace in the hole is sincerity. Thanks to their mirror neurons, your child's brain will register that your efforts are genuine, leading to a release of calming neurochemicals regardless of how well you follow the exact structure provided.

Sample Script: "You Just Don't Get it!"

CHILD: "You just don't get it!"
PARENT: "It must feel like I really don't get how important the game is to you."

CHILD:	"Well, you don't!"
PARENT:	"I'd be angry too in your shoes. You have a lot of fun with it and I probably don't understand all the parts of it."
CHILD:	"So why don't you just let me play, then?! My friends are all online and they're allowed."
PARENT:	"Yeah, I guess it feels crappy to have to miss out. Technology really is more social than it used to be when I was a kid. It makes sense that you'd want to keep playing to be with them too. Okay – let's talk about this at dinner tonight so we can find a solution that works. We're not going to let you play non-stop, but we can figure something out."
CHILD:	"Fine."

Common Pitfalls

1. "But I really don't 'get it.'" Fair enough. We're not often going to understand our kids completely. Here's a trick: validating the fact you don't actually get it and how that's frustrating to them is actually "getting it," at least the most important part of it. Conveying understanding of their frustration with you may be enough to break the ice and lead to more connection. It may even open the door to your child trying to tell you more of what's going on. Your child will also appreciate you trying to understand better, especially if this is a new way of relating to each other.

2. "My parents never fully understood me, and I turned out fine." This is true for lots of us. Thankfully, full understanding isn't possible or necessary. The main component of understanding here is really seeing that the child's motivations are inherently normal and good. In the extreme situation, when children feel rejected by their parents, this has a profound impact on the emotional health and well-being of all involved. As professionals, we see this often with 2SLGBTQ+ children, teens, and adults and their loved ones. If gender identity or sexual orientation is a relevant topic for your family, let us first acknowledge that this is new territory for so many adults in caregiving roles. Even if you don't understand fully your child's experience or identity, making an effort to educate yourself can show that even if you don't quite get it yet, you care deeply about getting to know them better. In fact, when parents make the effort to learn more about their children's inner world more generally, it leads to more connection for everyone involved, even if there is a road ahead in terms of the understanding piece. In this domain, effort really does count twice.

What might make it hard for me to put into words my child's experience in a situation like this?

_____

_____

_____

What might make it hard for me to get practical in a situation like this?

_____

_____

_____

What do I need to deal with a situation like this more confidently in the future?

_____

_____

_____

Scenario B: "You'll Never Understand"

Your child wants to participate in an event scheduled during an important religious or cultural celebration. It's very important to you that your children honor their tradition. When you say he can't go to the event, he says, under his breath: "You'll never understand."

The Knee-Jerk Response

Much of the time, parents and caregivers will respond with something like:

"Come on, it won't be that bad. You can see your friends another time."

"The whole family is going; this is nothing new."

Sometimes, especially when frustrated, one might say:

"You need to respect your traditions!"

Imagine for a moment that your child says to you her version of "You'll never understand."

What's your most likely knee-jerk response?

_____

_____

_____

 # Step 1. Building a Bridge

It's clear that family and community values are important. But what is the child's point of view? Children are usually focused on what they think will be most fun and can't see the wider importance of tradition. Especially if their family isn't from the dominant culture, they can feel like it's "weird" or embarrassing to do something their friends don't do. They may not know how to explain this to their peers. Children worry about being left out of their group of friends or seen as "different," especially as they reach middle childhood and preteen years. Children who grow up in a different culture from their parents often feel a bit misunderstood by both the dominant culture and their parents' cultural community. It can be quite lonely to straddle both worlds. They may have siblings or cousins who really "get it," but it's still difficult to have religious or cultural barriers between parent and child.

Possible Emotion Translations

Possibility A: "I'm worried that if I miss this event, I'll miss out on what my friends are doing, and being included is really important to me. You always say family matters most, but my friends count too. I'm worried that if I say that you'll just get mad at me."

Possibility B: "When you grew up, everyone went to this traditional festival, but here, no one even knows what it is. I'm worried it will make me look different and that feels vulnerable."

Possibility C: "It's hard for me to feel so different from you in this way. I'm not sure I believe what you believe, but I'm worried that if I don't accept your ways, you'll be really disappointed in me."

Translations for your child:

_____

_____

_____

⬭ Step 2. Putting It into Words

Option 1. "I get why you think I wouldn't understand. It seems like we're always dragging you to these events when you'd rather be with your friends. Your friends mean a lot to you and you don't want to miss out."

Option 2. "I understand that you think since Mom and I grew up in a different country/time, we can never really get what it's like to grow up here and now. It might feel like we can never really get what it's like to be you."

Option 3. "I can imagine it would feel pretty lonely when we go to these events. It's our world, but it's only partly your world."

In your own words:

I can imagine why you would feel we don't understand because _____, and because _____, and because _____.

 ## Step 3. Getting Practical

Emotional support: This is one of those situations where acknowledging your child's point of view may be the most important factor because the whole thing is about connecting through feeling more understood. It's also about accepting your children even if they are different from you and have a different point of view. Offering them comfort won't hurt either, so that they can feel your love across the current divide. You can also remind your child that feelings pass. The truth is, as much as we focus on attending to emotions, they rise and they fall and that can be really helpful for kids to know when they are at the peak of their "feelings mountain." Time really does help to feel better, whether inside or within the family or between friends, especially at this age. It's only if you lead with reassurance and perspective-giving that it will fall on deaf ears. The validation statements need to come first to open the door.

Practical support: Young children will, of course, need to follow along with their parents. As your child gets older, you may consider negotiating around some of your expectations. For example, you may allow your child to bring a friend along with the family or to meet up with their friends after the main part of the event. You may allow for missing certain family events as long as others are attended. If there are no points for negotiation around attendance, then maybe what the child does at the event can be negotiated.

Sample Script: "You'll Never Understand"

PARENT: "Saturday, we are going with the family to celebrate the holiday."

CHILD: "No, it's Ava's birthday party! Ugh! You'll never understand."

PARENT: "I get why you think I wouldn't understand. It seems like we're always dragging you to these events when you'd rather be with your friends. Your friends mean a lot to you and you don't want to miss out."

CHILD: "It's not just that! Ava is one of my best friends!"

PARENT: "It sounds important to you to be there for her. You don't want to let her down, and it would be really fun. It's pretty hard to have a holiday and an important birthday party on the same day."

CHILD: "I know the holiday matters too, but isn't there any way I can do both?"

PARENT: "Well, the holiday ends at sundown. I know it isn't perfect, but do you want me to drive you to Ava's after dinner?"

CHILD: "I guess it's better than nothing. What am I supposed to tell her?"

PARENT: "Well, let's figure that out together."

*Reminder: The proposed framework is not a magic formula. It can also feel really awkward since it goes against so much of what we were taught about how to respond to children's thoughts and feelings. We do urge you to try it out a few times following the steps as closely as possible as practice really does make a difference over time.

Common Pitfalls

1. "There is nothing to negotiate here." If a family tradition is extremely important, it may feel like there is no room to negotiate. There may never have been negotiation around issues in your family. Some children will get through adolescence going along with the family's tradition. It is more difficult when in a non-dominant culture because kids see their friends living very differently and feel misunderstood. When this happens, children can become more disconnected from parents emotionally, even if they are following the rules on the surface. They may feel angry and resentful or become more anxious and unhappy or complain of physical problems to get out of going with the family. Small amounts of negotiation can help kids feel more connected and onboard. It may not have been necessary or possible in your own family growing up, yet it may make a big difference in your child's sense of well-being today.

2. "This is disrespectful. He doesn't value our tradition." If you were raised in a family where children did not question or oppose parents' wishes, then asking to go to a birthday instead of a family holiday or religious event can seem very disrespectful. It can also feel like the child doesn't value the family's culture. This is already a fear many people have when moving to a new country or community, and the child rejecting the family culture can be a painful reminder. So, if you notice some anger (which is totally normal when we feel disrespected or rejected), take a moment to acknowledge this to yourself and be kind to yourself. It *is* painful when children don't appreciate the importance of our religion or culture. There may be quite a bit of grief, and you can't gloss over that. Then go back to step 1 of building a bridge to understand what your child's point of view may be. It is normal for children to think of their own self-interest first. This is a situation where it is helpful to recognize that the child's wish is not a wish against the parent. It is a difference in life experience and preferences and with time, it will be possible to smooth out these edges.

Reflections

What might make it hard for me to put into words my child's experience in a situation like this?

_____

_____

_____

What might make it hard for me to get practical in a situation like this?

_____

_____

_____

What do I need to deal with a situation like this more confidently in the future?

_____

_____

_____

Figure 12.1 Knee-jerk response

Figure 12.2 Validation and support

"I Can't Decide ..."   13

Kids get stuck for many reasons, and one of them is indecision. We've seen many kids freeze, shut down, and meltdown because they are overwhelmed with choice or don't know what exactly to say or where to start. These days, there are so many products, clothes, and options in every department of life, it's no wonder choosing is often a source of distress. It doesn't help that their brain isn't the most flexible for much of childhood and adolescence, especially since when a child gets stuck, it can affect the whole family. If there's a major time crunch or the choice offered is unreasonable for your child's developmental level, then of course you may need to step in and choose for him. However, choice is part of growing up, and learning to make choices also builds confidence.

Scenario A: "I Can't Decide ..."

Let's say a child has to pick a small toy at the dentist or a color of an ice pop at a birthday party, and he gets overwhelmed with the choices in front of him. He says to his parent, "I can't decide ..."

The Knee-Jerk Response

Much of the time, parents and caregivers will respond with something like:

"Hurry – just choose the one you like better."

"I think you should just pick the red one."

Sometimes, especially when frustrated, one might say:

That's it. If you can't choose, I'll do the choosing for you or you won't get to have one.

Imagine for a moment that your child says to you his version of "I can't decide ..."

What's your most likely knee-jerk response?

_____

_____

_____

 ## Step 1. Building a Bridge

Decisions are hard! It actually takes a lot of mental energy to make choices and the more options we have, the more stressed we can become. We have often been taught that making decisions is a logical process, but decisions are often made on an emotional level, at least to some degree. Kids who have a harder time tuning into their own emotions and body sensations can have a harder time choosing. More empathic, perceptive, perfectionistic, or anxious kids may also fear making a choice that displeases their caregiver or isn't the "best choice." FOMO affects kids too (Don't remember what that means? Ask your kids – they will be happy to educate you as we were educated ☺).

Possible Emotion Translations

Possibility A: "I like how cool the sticker looks, but I'm worried that if I choose it, I'll regret it because it won't last as long as the dinosaur."

Possibility B: "I want the chocolate ice pop but I know adults think a fruit popsicle is better. I don't want anyone to be disappointed in me."

Possibility C: "I'm overwhelmed because I just can't tell which one I want and I definitely can't do it fast. My brain is too full of pros and cons."

Translations for your child:

_____

_____

_____

Step 2. Putting It into Words

Option 1. "It *is* a tough choice! You like so many of them and don't want to feel like you picked the wrong one."

Option 2. "Yeah, it would be easier if they just had one color, so you wouldn't have to pick! It's so hard to know which will be the best."

Option 3. "I bet you can imagine having every one of them – it might be hard to settle on just one, especially if you are feeling pressured."

In your own words:

I can imagine why you would have a hard time choosing because _____, and because _____, and because _____.

*Reminder: Your child's brain will be far more open to your emotional and practical support, including the setting of limits, when you first put into words their perspective.

Step 3. Getting Practical

Emotional support: Having trouble choosing is a common experience for so many kids, especially younger ones. Once you've put into words their experience as just described, you may want to just be with your child patiently while they manage their own choice process. Tolerating doubt (did I pick the best one or not?) and uncertainty ("what if I'm upset with what I chose?") are skills we teach our children through our calm presence. We can communicate that it's normal to have a hard time choosing and that you believe in their ability to make a good choice. You can also let them know that you are for them in case they want your help to work it through.

Practical support: When possible, we suggest resisting the urge to force a choice immediately or pick for the child. We want children to have the opportunity to work through the dilemma. However, no one has all day to wait around, and if they are really stuck, it helps kids to have clear limits as to how long they can take. Reducing the number of choices to a smaller unit (e.g. offer only 2 instead of 4 options) may also be necessary. If the child is really out of sorts, you might encourage taking a temporary break from the decision by redirecting him to something else, like a game or another activity.

A note on choice: A little choice is helpful for kids; too much choice can really increase anxiety. If at all possible, we suggest giving two or at most three choices to young children, and only about things that make sense. For example, asking a child to choose the family's activity for the day or what to eat for dinner is usually much too difficult a decision. Sometimes, caregivers hope that letting the child decide what she wants to do will make her happy, but more often than not, the pressure that results has the opposite effect. As kids get older, they can be engaged in family decision-making and have input (this is really helpful in the older childhood and preteen years), but always in the way that makes sense for their age and developmental level. For example, a child who starts restricting her eating will need parents to step back in and choose meals for her until she's able to make good choices once more.

Sample Script: "I Can't Decide …"

You're at an open house for your stepchild's new daycare, and she is presented with a bucket full of stickers and toys to choose from. She looks up at you with worry in her eyes and says:

CHILD: "Hena, I can't decide!"
PARENT: "It *is* a tough choice! They all look like fun and you don't want to feel like you picked the wrong one."
CHILD: "Uhuh. I want the sticker and the frog and the ruler."
PARENT: "I bet you do – it's really hard to imagine only choosing one when they all look so cool."
CHILD: "Yes! I just don't know which one to pick!"
PARENT: It's so hard! You don't want to be upset with your choice. I know you can figure this out and I can help. Well, you already have a ruler at home, and so why don't you pick between the sticker and the frog. Stickers are fun and flashy, but the frog will last longer. What do you think?
CHILD: "Frog."
PARENT: "You did it! Great job deciding! Okay, let's go see your dad. What are you going to name your new little buddy?"

Common Pitfalls

1. "I don't want to stress my child out over something so small."
There is truth to this. It won't always be worth it to work this type of
thing through. The issue is that when some kids get to routinely avoid
decision-making, it can keep the avoidance going and they come to
rely on others around them to make decisions. It's much easier to practice occasional decision-making with a stuck child when young than
have to tame the beast later. The stress will only really lessen with practice and seeing that everything was okay after making the choice or
at least not that bad! That being said, we encourage you to pick your
battles. If you've got a lot going on, it may not be time for this kind of
coaching.

**2. "Are you really suggesting we use a strategy for such a minor
issue?"** Remember in the first part of the book when we talked about
the rationale for this kind of approach? Not only does it help to increase
cooperation and decrease the likelihood of a meltdown in the moment,
it also supports the development of brain structures that are responsible
for coordinating emotion and rational thought. Every time you use the
approach, you are supporting brain growth between the parts of the
brain that work together to make choices and to regulate big feelings.
This means that interactions like these – even if they aren't necessarily a
big deal – serve to build and strengthen your child's capacity to tolerate
stress in a variety of contexts and situations. And so, in a way, you can
think about it as an awesome investment in your child's development of
very worthwhile abilities.

Reflections

What might make it hard for me to put into words my child's experience
in a situation like this?

_____

_____

_____

What might make it hard for me to get practical in a situation like this?

_____

_____

_____

What do I need to deal with a situation like this more confidently in the future?

_____

_____

_____

Scenario B: "I Just Don't Know Which One to Choose!"

Let's say an older child has a school assignment with a list of 10 topics she can select from. She's been stuck, staring at the paper for an hour. On the verge of tears, she says, "I just don't know which one to choose!"

The Knee-Jerk Response

Much of the time, parents and caregivers will respond with something like:

"Just pick any one. I'm sure you'll do well."

"Well, you like sports, so why don't you do that sports one?"

Sometimes, especially when frustrated, one might say:

"It's not that hard, just make a decision!"

Imagine for a moment that your child says to you her version of "I just don't know which one to choose!"

What's your most likely knee-jerk response?

_____

_____

_____

Step 1. Building a Bridge

Imagine you are offered three jobs in your field. They are slightly different, and each comes with unique advantages and disadvantages. Which one to pick? If you're like me you might ask people for advice or you might create a spreadsheet, ranking each job on various factors to compare them in more detail. You might even ask for more time to decide. When we call an example like this to mind – and then morph it into an example with your child and their unique way of being in the world – we can more easily imagine what it's like for them to pick from a list of 10 topics for something that might feel really important to them. In their little world, everyday choices do feel like big decisions, and it can help them to navigate these dilemmas when we acknowledge their stress and support them through it.

Possible Emotion Translations

Possibility A: "I'm worried that if I pick the wrong one, I'll get a bad mark, and I won't be able to handle my anxiety and shame over that."

Possibility B: "If I pick the wrong one, it may be too hard, and then I'll never get it done. And I don't want to regret my choice – that's a bad feeling too."

Possibility C: "What if my teacher doesn't like the essay I write and thinks I'm stupid?"

Translations for your child:

_____

_____

_____

*Reminder: The idea here is to connect with your child's good intentions, vulnerable feelings, or need for connection driving his current state of being, even if on the surface it doesn't seem so.

Step 2. Putting It into Words

Option 1. "It's really hard to choose between so many topics, especially when you think you need to pick a certain topic to do well."

Option 2. "No wonder this list is giving you a hard time! You like to do your best to make your teacher happy and it must be tough to know which one she'll like."

Option 3. "I can imagine it's a lot of pressure to choose only one topic. You might worry you'll regret not choosing the other one and get stuck on that."

In your own words:

I can imagine why you'd feel stuck about which to choose because _____, and because _____, and because _____.

 Step 3. Getting Practical

Emotional support: Similar to the previous scenario, children in this situation need your trust that they can figure out some of their problems independently. They also need to learn to manage the anxiety and uncertainty that are part of school and life. We recommend conveying to them your confidence in their capacity to manage whatever comes up, regardless of their decision. It may also be helpful to remind them that making choices is a way to learn about ourselves, and so regardless of their choice they will be better equipped the next time. If your child does feel regret, you can remind her that (1) the feeling will pass, (2) we can use regret to learn about what's really important to us, and (3) we can never predict or know exactly what is going to happen, but we can have faith in our ability to cope with whatever happens.

Practical support: As in the scenario just described, many children who ask for help with decision-making don't actually *need* practical support. More often, what they need is the emotional support to calm their brain from the stress of the decision so that they can think more clearly about what to do. For those who do need a little help in the practical domain, you can consider going through the options with them and having the child notice which ones *feel* more appealing. It's less about thinking it through and more about noticing which topics bring out the child's natural sense of interest, curiosity, or enthusiasm. For example, you can suggest to your child that he imagine he's chosen a topic and is about to write about it and then ask: "how does it feel?" You can ask more specifically what the child notices in his body. It may take a few moments and a few deep breaths to tune into sensations, especially for a child who isn't used to doing so, but it's worth the effort. Our bodies are extremely reliable sources of information on how we feel. For example, if he notices a heaviness or tightness with one topic but lightness or calm with another, then he'll have his answer. Once kids are able to tune in to their gut reaction and trust it, the decision-making process becomes much more straightforward. There is also the traditional approach of helping you child create a list of pros and cons or brainstorming where he may get the information he needs to make a decision. It usually helps to do a little bit of research on a couple of the choices to see what you like more, but many kids will need some prompting to figure out the smaller steps to do so.

Sample Script: "I Just Don't Know Which One to Choose!"

You walk past your child's bedroom and notice her head down on her desk when she's supposed to be doing homework. When you ask what's wrong she says:

CHILD: "My teacher gave us this paper! I just don't know which one to choose!" (flings the paper in your direction – you see it's a list of 10 topics for an opinion essay)

PARENT: "Oooh! That's a lot of choice. None of them probably seem very appealing, huh?"

CHILD: "I don't even know what they mean!"

PARENT: "Well, let's look at these ones. You start to read: 'Impact of social media on kids' …"

CHILD: "Mom! They're all stupid! You don't need to read them!"

PARENT: "Okay, I get it now. It's stressful to have to choose one of these topics because you want to do well and because it's hard to tell which one is going to go best."

CHILD: "I don't know anything about 'Paper vs. Plastic' or any of these things."

PARENT: "It's so tough to choose when you don't think you know enough about the topics, and you don't want to waste time on one that won't work out. Let's look up a couple of them to see."

CHILD:	"But then how do I pick?"
PARENT:	"Well, I've seen you choose projects you like before, and I'm sure you can do it now. You know what you're interested in and a little pre-research might do the trick."
CHILD:	"But what if the teacher doesn't like it?"
PARENT:	"I get why you'd worry about her opinion because she marks the essay and you want to do well. Do you think she'd give these topics if she weren't okay with them?"
CHILD:	"I guess not. Okay, well I'll look at them again. Can you look at them with me?"
PARENT:	"I've got to get dinner ready. Why don't you have a go first? It's your topic and I trust you to figure out one that's good enough."
CHILD:	"Fine."
CHILD:	(30 minutes later, yelling from upstairs) "Mom, I'm going to do it on women who've won the Nobel Prize."
PARENT:	"Glad you figured it out! Should be interesting too – you could teach me a thing or two."

Common Pitfalls

1. "But I want her to do well. She might choose something she can't handle." Standing by and watching your child make a less than great decision is one of the most difficult things to do as a parent. We have so much experience and wisdom (often learned the hard way) that we want to share with our children. When we see them making a choice we wouldn't make or that might make life harder (for her and for us), it's natural to want to help steer the ship in a better direction. Children can pick up on the parent's strong desire to shape the process, and while they may follow along in the short term, it can make it more difficult for the child to trust her own instincts in the long-term. As you give her more opportunity to make her own mistakes, you may be surprised to find her becoming more decisive and feeling proud of her growing competence.

2. "It's important to meet real-world expectations." There can be a sense that kids today are being taught to over-focus on doing what they feel is right for them. While we certainly believe in the importance of "following your heart," it is both useful and important to help children consider other perspectives too. After all, maybe the teacher really does prefer students do their science experiment on a legitimate chemical reaction and not how long you have to chew gum for it to lose its flavor. Decisions may also need to be in the best interest of the team, group or community. Decision-making can lead to a discussion about what the child values. In our experience, when helped to explore their own thoughts and feelings about the possible outcomes, most kids will make positive choices that benefit both themselves and others.

Reflections

What might make it hard for me to put into words my child's experience in a situation like this?

_____

_____

_____

What might make it hard for me to get practical in a situation like this?

_____

_____

_____

What do I need to deal with a situation like this more confidently in the future?

_____

_____

_____

"Don't Go to Work!" 14

The ultimate trigger (at least for us): "Don't go to work!" Can you feel that visceral response bubbling below the surface? And when it happens, it can sometimes seem like kids are being overly dramatic or even bossy, which doesn't make it any easier to stomach. In our experience, this isn't intentional "manipulation" or "controlling" but trying to influence a situation that's causing them stress in the best way they know how. Sometimes the worry they experience makes them feel uncomfortable in their bodies (for more on this topic, refer to the Chapter 9: "My tummy hurts …") whereas other times it's a mask for anger they may not feeling comfortable expressing – especially toward the person they want around them the most.

Scenario A: "Don't Go to Work!"

Let's say you're getting ready to go to an evening work function. You're getting dressed and your child bursts into the room and flops onto your bed exclaiming: "Please don't go to work!"

The Knee-Jerk Response

Much of the time, parents and caregivers will respond with something like:

"Sweetie, be a big boy and go play – mommy needs to go to work tonight."

"You'll be fine, Grandma will take good care of you!"

Sometimes, especially when frustrated, one might say:

"You didn't seem to care all afternoon when you were playing outside!"

Some parents may even try to sneak out the door, so as not to cause too much of a fuss.

Imagine for a moment that your child says to you his version of "Don't go to work!"

What's your most likely knee-jerk response?

_____

_____

_____

 ## Step 1. Building a Bridge

Children depend on their parents for a sense of safety and security. Many feel a little uncomfortable with separation well into adolescence. Some kids, those with a more anxious temperament or those who may have experienced more stress in the past, may even become quite anxious or angry when primary caregivers are away for a period of time. They may feel like you don't care about them or they may worry that they will be flooded with sadness or that something bad might happen to them or to you. Younger children also don't have a very good sense of time so it can be difficult for them to understand what to expect.

*Reminder: First, try to guess the context: Did something just happen recently? Does your child have a pattern of getting upset in similar situations? They key is to ask yourself: what is the most vulnerable explanation for my child's complaint?

Possible Emotion Translations

Possibility A: "I'm going to miss you too much and that feeling is too big for me!"
Possibility B: "I don't want something bad to happen to you or me."
Possibility C: "I'm mad that you have to leave again."

Translations for your child:

_____

_____

_____

 ## Step 2. Putting It into Words

Option 1. "No wonder you don't want me to go. I can imagine you're worried that you'll miss me and it might be hard without me there to help you with the sad feelings."

Option 2. "It must feel like it will be too long before you see me next. And maybe you're scared something bad might happen while I am away. I get that you wish I could stay with you instead."

Option 3. "I bet you're mad at Mommy for leaving again. I can imagine it doesn't feel good that work is so important."

In Your Own Words:

I can imagine why you wouldn't want me to go to work because _____, and because _____, and because _____.

*Reminder: It's important not to stop here. Getting practical is essential for anxious kids; otherwise validating their experience can keep them stuck in a loop of worry. Putting in words their experience creates the brain flexibility that will be helpful for the next steps.

 ## Step 3. Getting Practical

Emotional support: Kids need to feel safe and cared for even when their main caregiver isn't around. Most of the time, showing your confidence in the alternate care provider is the strongest way to help your child feel safe. The message here is: "I trust this person." They also need to feel secure in your relationship even when you aren't there. They need to know that out of sight doesn't mean out of mind and that you are still thinking about them even if you aren't present in the same room. Finally, expressing your confidence in your child's realistic ability to manage goes a long way. You might say something like, "I was so impressed with how last time I went out, you read a story to your stuffies" or "I know that since you're getting older you're going to find it even easier this time to spend the evening with grandpa." Refocusing from your child's anxieties to your child's capacity helps him shift focus too. You might also remind your child that feelings *do* eventually pass (they really do rise and fall!). A few minutes of 1:1 time can also ease the transition.

Practical support: If your child struggles with anxiety about separating from you, in addition to some reassurance that they are safe, they also need help to face their fear in ways appropriate for their age. Whether it's a daycare drop-off, taking the bus for the first time or a birthday party, separation fears will happen at some time for most children. Planning ahead of time can make things much easier. Here are some things to consider ahead of the separation:

1. Tell children the truth. As tempting as it may be to sneak away while they are happy or to tell a white lie, children become more anxious if and when they realize they've been deceived. They will expect to be deceived in the future, which will increase their vigilance.
2. Practice with small separations first and gradually work your way up to the bigger ones.
3. Show your confidence in your child's ability to handle the separation. As you prepare them, use positive language like "You and your babysitter are going to have so much fun," or "Let's plan some extra special things you can do with Papa on Friday night." Minimize checking and questioning like "Are you worried?" and "Are you sure you're going to be okay?"

Even if you've done all you can to prepare your child, the anxiety will still surface some of the time. In these instances, you will still need to support your child by ensuring a trusting handover to the other responsible adult, perhaps even using rewards for steps in the right direction, and staying the course. In other words, it is just as important to remain consistent and firm with respect to the plan as it is to be comforting.

Sample Script: "Don't Go to work!"

CHILD: "Don't go to work, Mommy!"

PARENT: (turns to child, gets down to her level and holds her hands) "Oh, sweet pea. It's not fair that I have to go to work and you don't get to come."

CHILD: (turns away) "It isn't fair! I don't want you to go. I'm mad at you."

PARENT: "I think sometimes you worry it will be too long before you see me and that makes you really upset. I bet you wish that it could just be me and you all day long."

CHILD: "I don't even know when you're coming home."

PARENT: "Right – that's a yucky feeling! Well you do know that Mommy always comes to get you from daycare, and we walk home together. I come after 2:30. How about I show you how to know that time on the clock? But even if I'm a little after that, I'll always come."

CHILD: "Okay, Mommy."

PARENT: "Let's have a big hug. Let's get your backpack ready and you can tell me about the rocket ship you are making."

Common Pitfalls

1. "I'm a terrible parent. Maybe I shouldn't go back to work?" It's pretty hard as a parent to escape the pressure to give 100% to our children and to work and to be social and to take care of ourselves, and, and, and … This is extra hard in separated families where there may be less day-to-day time with kids. Despite making the best choices possible, many parents still feel badly about being torn in several directions. If you can relate, go back to Chapter 4 to practice the strategies for self-compassion. It will make it so much easier to stand back and not take this comment personally. When it comes to caregiving, research has shown time and time again that quality matters more than exact quantity. We can all experience shame as parents and worry that we aren't doing enough for our children. We need to recognize when these feelings pop up so we don't let them make our parenting decisions for us. Kids may complain when you go out, but they benefit from seeing their parents happy and fulfilled too. There needs to be a balance within your current reality – whatever that may be.

2. "I miss my kiddos too, and I definitely worry about their well-being when I'm not with them." Some of us really want the extra time with our kids and worry they may feel alone or left behind. This is especially difficult if we've ever felt that way in our own childhoods. If you can relate to that feeling, it's possible that every time you leave your child, you relive your own pain. Even if you say nothing, kids have antennae to pick up on caregivers' fears. It becomes a cycle in which a child seems anxious about separation, so then the parent becomes more anxious and then the child, sensing that, becomes more anxious still. Caregivers can take the lead in breaking this cycle by setting a step-by-step plan to gradually increase separation and showing kids this is okay. There are great books and websites in the appendix that explain how to do this. Having brief separations from parents is a vital part of development for older kids. As they master some independent time, you'll also see kids' confidence and sense of mastery grow.

3. "I don't want to damage our attachment." Some books and websites about "attachment" seem to suggest that it is harmful for children to experience distress when separated from their parents. Of course we don't want to cause our children harm and kids who have separation fears can be in a lot of distress, reinforcing the idea that leaving them temporarily can cause damage. Our best research information on attachment suggests that while appropriate care and comfort are essential to a child's well-being, developing emotional health requires a balance of closeness and separateness between parent and child. Healthy attachment is about being there for comfort as much as it is helping them to let go for periods of time. When children have enough of their primary attachment figures and good quality support at daycare, school, or other environments, they do well. In other words, they don't need their main caregivers all the time, especially after age 5 or 6. This means that it's absolutely, totally, 100% okay to be away from your child for periods of time. In fact, what can be more important to the child's adjustment is whether their emotions about the separation are expressed and worked through.

Reflections

What might make it hard for me to put into words my child's experience in a situation like this?

_____

_____

_____

What might make it hard for me to get practical in a situation like this?

_____

_____

_____

What do I need to deal with a situation like this more confidently in the future?

_____

_____

_____

Scenario B: "You Care More about Your Job than You Do about Me!"

Your child made the basketball team this year. He's really excited about it, and every Wednesday evening his team plays another team in the school district – the same day you lead a weekly staff meeting. You can make arrangements once in a while to get coverage to see him play but not as often as you (or he) would like. Another Tuesday night rolls around, and your son asks you if you'll be coming to his game, and you give him the bad news. He turns around and walks away, muttering under his breath: "You care more about your job than you do about me."

The Knee-Jerk Response

Much of the time, parents and caregivers will respond with something like:

"That's just not true. How can you say that?"

"You are very important to me, but the meetings were already scheduled."

Sometimes, especially when frustrated, one might say:

"Someone needs to pay for the roof over your head, never mind your sports equipment that cost me over a hundred dollars!"

Imagine for a moment that your child says to you her version of "You care more about your job than you do about me!"

What's your most likely knee-jerk response?

_____

_____

_____

⌒ Step 1. Building a Bridge

This is one of those accusations that can really sting. Some parents really take it to heart; others might find it over the top. It depends on you, your child, and the context. In any case, it will likely take a moment to check in with yourself about your reaction before building the bridge to understand your child's point of view. Usually when kids level this accusation or complaint, they are feeling left out, are missing you, or are disappointed about missing out on something else because you are not available. They often hide their sadness in anger.

Possible Emotion Translations

Possibility A: "When you spend so many hours at work, I miss seeing you but I'm too embarrassed to admit it."

Possibility B: "I would love to have you at my basketball game, and I'm angry at you and your work for making that impossible."

Possibility C: "I'm sad because even if I don't show it, your approval, time, and attention mean a lot to me. I worry that I'm not worth it to you."

Translations for your child:

_____

_____

_____

*Reminder: The idea here is to connect with your child's good intentions, vulnerable feelings, or need for connection driving their current state of being, even if on the surface it doesn't seem so.

Step 2. Putting It into Words

Option 1. "I don't blame you for being angry at me, because work got in the way again. You want me to show more interest, and it's got to hurt when I don't show up."

Option 2. "You have every right to be upset. You really needed my support and I wasn't there. It must have felt like you didn't matter. I'd feel bad too if I were in your shoes."

Option 3. "I can imagine that it's probably a little bit embarrassing when your friends' parents are there and we're not. Maybe you feel awkward explaining why we aren't there. I bet that's upsetting too."

In Your Own Words:

I can imagine why you wouldn't want to be at work because _____, and because _____, and because _____.

 ## Step 3. Getting Practical

Emotional support: This scenario is a little different from the first one in this chapter. In the former, the parent is consistently there and the child is mostly anxious; in the latter, there has been a disappointment, and the child is angry and hurt rather than worried. Although it isn't realistic or helpful for parents to always put their children first, if you feel comfortable doing so, it can help to apologize for the hurt. You may also want to reassure your child with your words and actions that you love him, want to connect with him, and that he matters to you. Each of us has a different way of showing this. For some people, this may be verbal – for example, saying something like the preceding sentences and then adding "I wish I could have been there. I love to see you in action."

Practical support: This type of complaint may signal that the child feels there's a lack of quality time. We can all be busy and distracted such that we don't spend much time truly together. If you can relate, you may want to take some responsibility for the lack of connection and offer a realistic way to course-correct the feelings with a special date or a plan for next time. The good news is that it doesn't take much in the way of absolute time to strengthen the bond with a child. Even as little as 30 minutes of undivided attention a week has been shown to strengthen the parent–child relationship. This is like putting money in the emotional bank. A child will tolerate separation and missed commitments better if she feels like he is getting enough connection on a routine basis.

A note on new partners and remarriage: For those of you in new relationships, you may also hear "you care more about (your new partner) than you do about me!" This can be painful as you try to juggle everyone's feelings and can't seem to please anyone. It may also be relevant to go back to the Chapter 7: "You love my sister more …" and to reread the earlier section of this chapter substituting *new partner* for *work*. Kids desperately value 1:1 time with their parents; new partners and family members often change that dynamic. It's not a question of right or wrong (parents are allowed to find love and happiness for themselves) but of openly acknowledging the child's perspective and feelings about the change. The good news is that you don't actually need to clone yourself, but rather attend to your loved ones' feelings and to support them over the hump of hurt.

Sample Script: "You Care More about Your Job than You Do about Me!"

CHILD: "You care more about your work than you do about me!"

PARENT: "I don't blame you for being angry at me, because I promised to be there as often as I could and work got in the way again. I get why it would seem like I don't care."

CHILD: "That's lame, dad. Don't try to agree with me."

PARENT: "It may seem lame if it feels like I'm just trying to say what I think you want to hear. You have every right to be upset. All you want is for your father to pay attention and show interest, and it's got to hurt when I don't show up."

CHILD: "The science fair was a big deal. We got second prize. Jack's dad was there and he's the president of his company!"

PARENT: "Ouch. That would have made it extra hurtful. It might feel like I should have made it happen too. I wish I could have been there, and I would really love to see the project and hear all about the fair."

CHILD: "Well, you're probably too busy."

PARENT: "I am often busy, but I've got a couple hours tonight after dinner, and I'll turn off my phone so no one can interrupt us. Your brother can watch a video."

CHILD: "Fine, we'll see if you know anything about digestion" (smiling).

PARENT: "Does burping count?"

Common Pitfalls

1. "Aren't they too old for this kind of behavior?" It may feel too "needy" or "clingy" for an older child to ask for more attention. Similar to what we discussed earlier, the main emotional need here is one of connection with the parent and to feel like they matter. These are totally normal human needs. Depending on how we were raised, it may feel excessive or clingy, but in fact, adults throughout life need connection with their significant others. Also, the more children feel their parent pulling away, the more "clingy" they will become. This is the natural pattern in relationships. You may find that a little more 1:1 time is all it takes for things to settle down. And if you find yourself struggling with the boredom that often comes with kid-related activities, try to find something that would be enjoyable for both of you.

2. "My job is really important. My child needs to understand that." This is 100% true, and over time, your child will absolutely be able to look back and understand the logic of you being temporarily unavailable or away for periods of time. The thing is that children just don't have that perspective when they are children. Their brains aren't yet mature enough to handle that kind of big picture stuff. It's also normal for them to see their own needs as most important; believe it or not, that's not abnormal selfishness, it's developmental. It will help them to understand logically the importance of your work (or new partner) if you can first acknowledge that their emotional reaction to your being away is normal and acceptable. In fact, it's a compliment to you as a person and your relationship that they value you and want you around. It may come out as criticism, but it's actually an expression of love.

3. "I show my kid that he matters is so many ways. This feels disingenuous." As parents, we can't even keep track of the many ways we care for our children and put them first. If they only knew the extent of the sacrifice that comes with being a parent. It can feel silly to need to reassure a child about your commitment to him, but it's common for kids to worry about whether a parent is really there for them or even cares. This is the most important concern for most kids, so they continually test it and ask about it. Parents may have many connections, a partner, other kids, family members etc., but no one is more important to a kid than his parents.

Reflections

What might make it hard for me to put into words my child's experience in a situation like this?

_____

_____

_____

What might make it hard for me to get practical in a situation like this?

_____

_____

_____

What do I need to deal with a situation like this more confidently in the future?

_____

_____

_____

"I Got a Terrible Mark ..." 15

Because school is a big part of children's lives, so is classroom achievement. It's no secret that within each classroom there is a range of abilities, with about 50% of students performing in the average range, 25% performing better than their peers, and 25% struggling to keep up. By about the second grade, kids also start to recognize and care about how they are the same or different from their classmates, and they compare themselves to their peers to learn about themselves and the world. This means that when they struggle to succeed, it can feel even worse if they are also aware that they find themselves in the bottom of the grade pile. Unlike hobbies, where if you don't have natural talent or interest you can move on to another, school is a non-negotiable – and for a long time. Therefore, when kids struggle with performance, it's important to help them work through the associated emotions so that they don't end up with low academic self-esteem or low motivation. If you are reading this and thinking to yourself: "Too late! My kid already hates school/thinks he's stupid" – don't despair. These strategies can help to turn the ship around. Bad feelings fuel low academic self-esteem and low motivation. When we can help kids move through feelings like frustration, shame or sadness, they spontaneously feel better about themselves *and* school.

In other cases, kids will feel like they did terribly on a test or an assignment when objectively, they did okay, even quite well. Many children struggle with perfectionism, and it almost always comes out related to schoolwork and grades. A child with perfectionistic tendencies has a keen ability to notice and focus on mistakes. She tends to be hard on herself and expect herself to avoid mistakes and displeasing others at all costs. We will tackle both situations in this chapter.

Scenario A: "I Got a Terrible Mark …" (F)

In this scenario, let's assume your son did poorly on a spelling test. When you get home from work and ask about his day, he begrudgingly admits that he failed his test, spelling only 9 words correctly out of 20. He is sulking in front of the TV and avoids eye contact.

The Knee-Jerk Response

Much of the time, parents and caregivers will respond with something like:

"Aw, sorry honey you'll do better next time."

"Well, now you know that we have to do more practice together after dinner."

Sometimes, especially when frustrated, one might say:

"Did you even try? What happened? Were you fooling around?"

Imagine for a moment that your child says to you her version of "I got a terrible mark …"

What's your most likely knee-jerk response?

_____

_____

_____

 Step 1. Building a Bridge

Shame. It's one of the most noxious human experiences. It's a really hard emotion to manage for adults – imagine for kids with underdeveloped brain structures for regulation! When people feel shame – no matter their age – the impulse is to withdraw (hide their mistakes) or attack (it's your/ the teacher's fault this happened). Poor grades inevitably trigger shame. Even if your child acts like she really doesn't care, there's a high chance she does. Children care much more about what parents and teachers think than they'd like to admit.

Possible Emotion Translations

Possibility A: "I feel embarrassed. I'm scared I'll never be good at spelling."

Possibility B: "I'm mad at myself, and I'm worried you will be too."

Possibility C: "I'm fed up. No matter how hard I try, I feel like I'll never succeed."

Translations for your child:

_____

_____

_____

⬭ Step 2. Putting It into Words

Option 1. **"**I can imagine that it feels pretty bad, especially if other kids did well on the test."

Option 2. "I bet you feel disappointed. Maybe you're even worried that you'll get in trouble."

Option 3. "It's probably feels lousy to have to think about it. Failing feels bad, even if it's something like a spelling test."

In your own words:

I can imagine why you would feel bad about your mark because _____, and because _____, and because _____.

 ## Step 3. Getting Practical

Emotional support: Whatever your child throws your way like anger ("it was a stupid test anyway!"), other-blame ("my teacher didn't even tell us about the test"), or denial ("what test? I didn't have a test"), underneath it all is shame. Humans will do anything to avoid shame, so it's no wonder that some kids routinely try to avoid discussing poor grades, lie about them, or avoid the work they worry they'll do poorly on. What they need is communication of acceptance. They want to know that school performance doesn't affect how much you love them or care about them. It definitely helps some children to tell them that your love for them is *not* conditional on academic performance, but they also read your facial expression and body language. This means that if you notice that your own stress, embarrassment, or frustration with your child keeps surfacing, that has to be addressed first or attempts to do things differently with your child will backfire.

Practical support: Once your child feels reassured (and this may take more than a minute), only then is it time to help him face the situation. You can help children to do this by looking over a test or assignment together, talking to the teacher, changing some expectations at school, getting extra academic help, or a combination of these options. Heads up – if you choose the first option, it will take some creativity to look over a failed test without overwhelming the child with bad feelings. Other tactics that can help are asking the child to teach you the material, modeling the right approach without putting them on the spot to demonstrate what they can't yet do, and playing a game with the content without directly looking at the "mistakes" on the test.

Sample Script: "I Got a Terrible Mark …"

PARENT: "Hey Jer. How was school today?"
CHILD: "Bad."
PARENT: "Why – what happened?"
CHILD: (avoids any eye contact) "I failed my spelling test."
PARENT: "Oh no. I bet that's pretty disappointing."
CHILD: "No. I hate spelling. A lot of other kids failed too."
PARENT: "In that case, I could imagine you might feel frustrated."
CHILD: "I do. The words were too hard. It wasn't fair."
PARENT: "Makes sense you'd be upset. Maybe it feels like you didn't get a fair shot to do well, and you want to get a decent grade. Maybe it just feels lousy to have to share your mark with me."
CHILD: "Well it's not the end of the world."
PARENT: "You're right, it's not. I'm glad you can see that."
CHILD: "So, wait – I'm not in trouble?"
PARENT: "No, son, you're not in trouble. The most important thing is to learn from the experience and move on. And I'm here to help. We can practice for the next spelling test together if you want.

Of course I'll do my best to make it tolerable – I can imagine practicing spelling words with your dad isn't very high on your bucket list." (smiling)

CHILD: "Thanks, Dad."

*Reminder: The proposed framework is not a magic formula. It can also feel really awkward because it goes against so much of what we were taught about how to respond to children's thoughts and feelings. We do urge you to try it out a few times following the steps as closely as possible as practice really does make a difference over time.

Common Pitfalls

1. "He needs to feel the sting so he'll work harder next time." You want him to learn his lesson so that he does better next time. After all, academic success is a buffer in life and you want him to be a productive member of society – for his own sake! Although your motivations are very good, we now know that kids are rarely motivated by a sense of failure or by shame or fear. Rather, these experiences can lead to a desire to withdraw and hide. Over time, your child might then be triggered to pull back when faced with more challenging situations, rather than pushing himself to try again. Your child might even become critical of the teacher or adopt the position that school sucks. Good news though: When you can use the structure we've outlined, you can help your child move through the tough feelings so that they don't interfere with his natural inclination to keep at it.

2. "He's not going to succeed in life if he can't manage in school." When a kid comes home with a low mark, it makes sense that it can trigger our own fears for his future. It puts pressure on us to figure out a solution, and that's hard too. The issue is that our fears for the future can become a huge weight on our kids' shoulders. We absolutely need to act to help our kids manage academically, but the worry can get in the way of productive action. If kids sense that you don't believe in them, it affects their confidence. So we need to find our own practical action plans and ways to believe in our kids' successful future.

3. "Well, then, it's time to buckle down and study harder." You may feel anxious about this setback and decide that your child needs to increase homework time to help him to do better. You may even consider a tutor. While doing so may be necessary, it is important to maintain a balance between structured time that involve expectations (homework and chores) and unstructured time. Research shows that free play/free time is linked to a range of positive outcomes in child development and an absence of adequate time for child-led activities may be contributing to higher rates of depression and anxiety seen in children and teens over the last decade. So if more time is needed on after-school academic enrichment, then some other expectations may have to be decreased so there is still enough time for relaxing and having fun.

Reflections

What might make it hard for me to put into words my child's experience in a situation like this?

_____

_____

_____

What might make it hard for me to get practical in a situation like this?

_____

_____

_____

What do I need to deal with a situation like this more confidently in the future?

_____

_____

_____

Scenario B: "I Got a Terrible Mark …" (A)

In this next scenario, your daughter calls you from school and bursts into tears. She is devastated that she only earned an 88% on her science project. She usually strives for an A+ in every subject and was hoping to win the science fair. Someone else in her class earned a 94%.

The Knee-Jerk Response

Much of the time, parents and caregivers will respond with something like:

"But honey – an A is a great mark! You should be proud of yourself. So many kids would be happy with that mark."

"Sweetie – you have to see the big picture. It's okay! It's more than okay!"

Sometimes, especially when frustrated, one might say:

"You're being ridiculous. Stop being so dramatic."

Imagine for a moment that your child says to you his version of "I got a terrible mark ..."

What's your most likely knee-jerk response?

_____

_____

_____

 # Step 1. Building a Bridge

At first glance – this reaction to an A seems outsized and over-the-top. You may wonder where your child got this skewed perspective or how she can be so hard on herself. Many kids today feel a pressure to succeed academically that goes beyond anything we felt as children. Sometimes, they sense that it's hard "out there" to get into good programs and get well-paying jobs and so it can feel like the stakes are high. Some kids base self-worth on achievement, so mistakes are seen as a sign that they aren't "good enough." Others are simply wired for perfectionism.

Possible Emotion Translations

Possibility A: "I'm worried this mark will bring down my grade and I won't be allowed to stay in the gifted program."

Possibility B: "My academic reputation means a lot to me. Being the best academically is part of my identity and so this feels really embarrassing."

Possibility C: "You are always so proud when I come home with a great mark. I'd rather put myself down than risk feeling your disappointment in me."

Translations for your child:

_____

_____

_____

*Reminder: If you are feeling stressed or overwhelmed, engaging in this mental exercise can be a real challenge. You might find that taking a break or a couple of deep breaths might make it easier to brainstorm possible emotional translations.

 ## Step 2. Putting It into Words

Option 1. "I can understand why you'd be upset with your mark. Doing really well at school is really important to you and you don't want us to think you're not capable."

Option 2. "I'm thinking that maybe you're scared that you'll lose you're A+ average that you've worked so hard to achieve. Especially since you have your sights set on an Ivy League school."

Option 3. "No wonder you're upset. You worked so hard on that project! You really gave it your all, and so I could understand that anything less than an A+ is hard to stomach."

In your own words:

I can imagine why you'd feel upset about your mark because _____, and because _____, and because _____.

 ## Step 3. Getting Practical

Emotional support: The first thing to do is to recognize the genuine pain your child may feel in this situation. On some level, there is probably shame about her degree of perfectionism also ("I shouldn't be so upset; what's wrong with me"), so part of the task is to really under-stand how deeply wounded she really is and to be with her in that experience.

Then – if you first felt tempted to reassure your child about their mark or your impulse was to help them to see that "it's not such a big deal," it's now time to do just that. Remember that showing your child that you are with them with validating statements makes it possible for them to internalize your supportive words and see the "big picture." The way they are thinking about their problem becomes a lot less rigid too.

Practical support: Believe it or not, the way to help kids with per-fectionistic tendencies is to help them to become more comfortable with making mistakes, including not knowing everything. You can do so by sharing your own experiences of imperfection, emphasizing any vulnerable feelings (anxious, embarrassed) that came alongside, and how you were able to use these experiences to learn about yourself and life. You may even make a point of highlighting when you don't know something or laughing at yourself with kindness when you make mistakes.

For parents who have children who can't help but put undue pressure on themselves, you may consider setting some limits around time spent on homework or participation in achievement focused extracurricular activi-ties. Just like too little focus on achievement can signal underlying fears and shame needing attention, so too can perfectionism and overachieve-ment. You may need to take the lead in setting time aside for slower paced activities, like time in nature, family meals, or time with friends. If you deter-mine limits are in fact required to protect your child from wearing out from overdrive, don't forget to use this framework to respond to your child's stress or distress that will likely result: "I don't blame for being angry with me about the limits because … because … because …"

Sample Script: "I Got a Terrible Mark …" (A)

CHILD: "I basically failed my project!"
PARENT: "Huh? Really? What mark did you get?"
CHILD: "An A. I know what you're going to say: "It's a great mark. I should be sooooo proud." (in a mocking tone)
PARENT: That is the way I've responded in the past hasn't it. You're right, it hasn't always been helpful. I was trying to make you feel bet-

ter and instead I just made you feel like you couldn't talk to me about your feelings.

CHILD: "Yup."

PARENT: "Well, I did miss the boat on this one in the past. But if I put myself in your shoes, I see very clearly why you'd be upset. You worked really hard on your project and you were really proud of what you came up with. And marks matter to you. Not just because they make you feel good but because you're known for your ability to do well at school. It's like a part of who you are. And so it's maybe a bit embarrassing when you earn anything less than an A+. And when I rush to reassure you, without at least acknowledging what it's like for you, it can feel really unhelpful. Because I think you already know that in the end, it's going to work out, but it still feels crappy to feel like you're off course and that's just as important to you right now."

CHILD: "Oooookayyyy."

PARENT: (with a laugh) "Bet you don't recognize me, do you?"

CHILD: "Not really, no."

PARENT: "Is that better?"

CHILD: "Only if you mean it."

PARENT: "Well that's the best part. I do mean it. An old dog *can* learn new tricks."

Common Pitfalls

1. "It's so illogical – isn't this feeding into it?" In the example where your school-age child is worried about getting into an Ivy league school, you may be very tempted to dismiss their feelings because they aren't exactly grounded in logic. In a way it doesn't make sense for them to worry so much about their grades when they've got a ways to go before they even reach high school. However, as we've illustrated throughout the book, your efforts to help to correct the reality won't be effective without first putting into words their perspective. Besides, once they learn to harness the power of their drive, it will likely serve them very well in the future.

2. "She's the one who wants to stay up late improving her project."
Children who are high achievers and perfectionistic are at risk of going
to extreme lengths to "do their best," to the point where it can go overboard. We've encountered many instances where kids who put all
their focus into school were at greater risk of breakdown once they
entered college because they simply couldn't deal with all the competing demands. These kids can also lose sight of the importance of
cultivating other areas of life, like their social relationships or leisure
activities. Although they may act like they *want* to be driven to perfectionism, it is usually more about feeling compelled to do things
to feel less anxious or better about themselves. When perfectionism
is causing distress or disturbing a child's life, parents can intervene,
just as they would with any other less socially acceptable or unhealthy
behavior.

Reflections

What might make it hard for me to put into words my child's experience
in a situation like this?

_____

_____

_____

What might make it hard for me to get practical in a situation like this?

_____

_____

_____

What do I need to deal with a situation like this more confidently in the
future?

_____

_____

_____

Figure 15.1 Knee-jerk response

Figure 15.2 Validation and support

"I Hate My Life!" 16

When kids make comments like "I hate my life!" they can be said with different levels of despair. Healthy and generally well-adjusted kids will routinely say something like this when very upset but so may kids who've really been struggling. If you have any sense that your child is truly despairing about life, then it's important to ask directly and specifically about whether he has any thoughts of wanting to harm himself. If you have any concerns that your child may have thoughts of suicide, you do need to get professional help on an urgent basis. You may also wish to refer to Chapter 24: Recommended Readings for links to additional resources. The rest of this chapter is intended for parents of kids who say "I hate my life!" or some version of that comment when you are confident there is no actual intent for the child to harm himself or end his life.

Scenario: "I Hate My life!"

Your 10-year-old son has been getting into lots of trouble lately. He's in a pattern of acting out in class and losing privileges. At home, he's often fighting with his younger siblings and you've been butting heads. To make matters worse, he just found out he didn't make the city's competitive baseball team. While walking by you in the hallway later that evening, he mutters under his breath, "I hate my life …"

The Knee-Jerk Response

Much of the time, parents and caregivers will respond with something like:

"You don't really mean that. You were just fine 5 minutes ago."

"What? You have a great life. Other kids would give anything for the life you have."

Sometimes, especially when frustrated, one might say:

"Too bad. You'll have to learn to make better choices then."

Imagine for a moment that your child says to you her version of "I hate my life!"

What's your most likely knee-jerk response?

_____

_____

_____

 ## Step 1. Building a Bridge

Think of the last time you said something dramatic. Maybe it was "I want a divorce!" Or "I swear I am quitting my job!" Connect with the part of you that can relate to feeling so overwhelmed that you couldn't see clearly for a moment and these phrases – or ones like them – popped out of your mouth. Now with that sentiment in mind, cross over to Upset Child Island and apply that blueprint over there. Saying that "I hate my life" often means feeling so upset that all systems are overloaded, with no ability to communicate something more rational. Even adults get stuck in believing that there is no way out of a terrible situation, especially when very upset and solutions seem non-existent. It is even more difficult for kids to have longer-term or "big picture" perspective. Your child isn't able to hold in mind how lucky they are in the overall scheme of the world; they are focused on their own immediate problem and don't see a solution.

Possible Emotion Translations

Possibility A: "I'm frustrated that I didn't make the baseball team. That was the one thing I thought might go well this year."

Possibility B: "I feel like nobody likes me anymore, not even you. I can't exactly come ask for a hug since we've been arguing non-stop."

Possibility C: "I am embarrassed for getting in trouble at school and now this let-down. It feels like I can't catch a break. The only way I can show you just how upset I really am is to tell you that I hate my life."

Translations for your child:

_____

_____

_____

⬭ Step 2. Putting It into Words

Option 1. "It must feel like everything's going wrong no matter how hard you try! No wonder you hate your life right now."

Option 2. "I wonder if you might be really disappointed about not making the team, and you want me to know just how upset you are."

Option 3. "Maybe it doesn't seem like I get how fed up you are. You really need me to know how serious this is."

In your own words:

I can imagine why you'd hate your life right now because _____, and because _____, and because _____.

*Reminder: Although these statements are meant to calm the storm in the brain, we don't want to stop there. If we did, it could feel like a bit of a cliffhanger. It's once you've reflected their experience that your child will be more open to your emotional and practical support.

Step 3. Getting Practical

In this scenario, it's important to help your child find more specific words for his feelings. Kids usually use these sweeping general statements ("I hate my life," "I hate you," or "nothing ever works out," etc.) when they can't make sense of their feelings.

Emotional support: Once you can break down their state of overwhelm into words using because-statements like in Step 2, you (and they) will start to feel better – even if just enough to see that there are solutions and better days ahead. For example, the child in this situation is likely experiencing a mixture of frustration, sadness and embarrassment.

Validating his feelings will likely help to diffuse them. Underneath it all, he likely also wants comfort. Sometimes kids are like porcupines, and it doesn't feel natural to offer a hug when they show their prickles, yet that may be exactly what they need. Children who say they hate their life also want to know that you take their feelings seriously, that you're in this together and that you have hope that things will get better. We can also reassure our children that no matter how big a problem, you will always love them, you will always be there with them, and the intensity they are feeling won't last forever.

If your child says he hates his life and you believe it's primarily because he's overwhelmed with shame at his own behavior and perceived failures, reassurance can help (check out Chapter 11: "I'm so Bad/Stupid …" for a refresher), and separating the problem behavior from the child's self-concept can help even more. One way to do this is to talk about the problem as something outside the child. This is called "externalizing the problem." Instead of the child being "bad" for disruptive behavior in class, you can talk about how the behavior itself is the problem and "takes over". Younger children like it when you make up a silly name (e.g., "squiggle-man") and vow to work with him together. For example: "When 'squiggle-man' shows up at the park, he's a lot of fun, but when he shows up at dinner, it can really upset the family. How can we all do something to help him?" Older kids still respond well to talking about the behavior as a separate entity. You might say: "Something has clearly been bugging you at school and getting you in trouble. Let's try to figure it out together."

Practical support: A potential strategy in this situation involves brainstorming ways your child can signal his upset to you earlier next time, before things go too far. Kids usually use these sweeping general statements ("I hate my life," "I hate you," or "nothing ever works out," etc.) when they can't make sense of their feelings. Once everyone is calm, you can practice other ways to communicate when really upset, like through drawing or learning more specific feeling words. It's also helpful to show the child how to think through the problem and possible solutions. For example, when the child first learns he didn't make the team, he may be so overwhelmed that he can't think of the other teams or activities he can sign up for. Once you've helped him sit with his disappointment for a long enough time to honor it, you can redirect him to consider a few other options and look at what he might enjoy in each. There is almost always a solution and almost always another opportunity.

A child who is more chronically seeing the world and her life as "glass half empty" can benefit from writing what she's grateful for each night before bed. This is a nice family activity that helps expand the focus on the good things. Volunteering or helping out in the neighborhood also builds appreciation in a way that just talking can't. Ultimately, most chil-

dren who say: "I hate my life" don't feel that way on a regular basis, and
once provided with some emotional support, they are able to remember
that things are actually going just fine.

A child who mentions hating their life frequently and with a lot of
distress may be in a different boat. They may be signaling that something in their life is feeling out of their control. Parents will then want
to get to the bottom of what else might be going on. For example, if a
child is in a difficult academic program and feeling overwhelmed or he
is being bullied at school, those issues need to be addressed head on
to help him feel better. Children have little control over their lives and
often don't recognize that there are options and so they don't always
think of asking for help. We also need to be willing to take an honest
look at the home environment for situations that feel to the child like
there's "no way out." Some situations where practical changes would be
needed include: when parents are in serious conflict (whether together
or separated), when experiencing any kind of mistreatment (including
repeated teasing by a sibling) and when a parent is seriously struggling
with mental health or substance use issues. If any of these are the case,
then the main problem will need to be addressed to lower the pressure
and sense of overwhelm felt by the child. Don't hesitate to reach out
for support. Dealing with any of these situations is highly stressful for
parents, and self-care strategies alone aren't usually enough.

Sample Script: "I Hate My life!"

Imagine a scenario where an 11-year-old girl gets placed in a class without any of her close friends. The next morning, she finishes the last muffin in a batch – the one her sister had been saving. Her father reprimands
her for her behavior:

PARENT: "June! Ruby was looking forward to that muffin. You should
have asked her."

CHILD: "Seriously? Ugh! I hate my life!" (storms off)

PARENT: (a few minutes later after taking some time to breathe) "Hey,
what you said before – sounds like you're pretty fed up with
everything."

CHILD: "Go away!"

PARENT: "I know things have been really hard at school with your new
class, and I get that you'd be super mad at me for making it
worse."

CHILD: "Duh!"
PARENT: "Well, it must feel like you can't get a break no matter what you do."
CHILD: "It's so unfair! How come Ruby never gets in trouble when she eats what I'm saving?"
PARENT: "Yeah, it must seem like I'm just blaming you and don't even notice what a bad day you're having."
CHILD: "You don't even seem to care that I'm with no friends. Not even one."
PARENT: "When all I focused on this morning was the muffin, you wondered if I even cared. No wonder you feel bad, because it seems so unfair and like I'm missing the real problem."
CHILD: "I can't go today, Dad! I can't!"
PARENT: "I know it's really hard to be in this new class without your friends at school. It's so bad that you don't want to go at all. Honey, it's totally normal to feel this way. This is a big change."
CHILD: "I don't, Dad."
PARENT: (gives a hug) "I really appreciate you telling me how you feel about what's really going. When you're ready, I'm here to help think of ways to deal with the situation. I'll check in again a bit later too."

Common Pitfalls

1. "If I pay a lot of attention to this kind of comment, won't he say it more?" Some parents worry that comments like these can lead us to a bit of a bottomless pit and that offering sympathy will only create more drama. What we've found is that kids who talk in more sensational terms often feel things very deeply and don't have a better way to ask for what they need (remember the concept of super-feelers in Chapter 9?). Unfortunately, ignoring it often leads to more dramatic language and escalation. Listening to his perspective and then helping to translate it into emotion words is the way to decrease the "drama." This is one where building a bridge is so important: It may take really having to imagine what it's like to be that age, in his body, in this world. We also don't encourage focusing on the words exclusively (e.g. "I hate my life!") because we want to focus on the feelings behind the words (e.g., sadness, shame, frustration, hopelessness) and other ways of expressing distress. So it's about the *kind of attention* you pay to the child. The middle ground is honoring the thoughts and feelings while redirecting the conversation to more helpful and realistic ways of communicating, and/or making practical changes if needed.

2. "Isn't this just being oversensitive?" It can be annoying to see your child upset about something that seems like a normal part of childhood for so many kids. Especially if we've had a hard day (or much bigger problems over the course of our own lives). It may be true that a child who has witnessed more of the human condition will be less likely to say he hates his life, but maybe not, since it's usually less about hating his actual life and more about being very upset with his current situation. Even when children do truly hate their own life, it is less a comparison or comment on anyone else's experience and more a reflection of how upset they are in general with themselves or their own particular situation. Thankfully, the biggest problem is not that life throws us curveballs, it's that sometimes the stress or distress that come alongside feels too much to bear alone.

Reflections

What might make it hard for me to put into words my child's experience in a situation like this?

_____

_____

_____

What might make it hard for me to get practical in a situation like this?

_____

_____

_____

What do I need to deal with a situation like this more confidently in the future?

_____

_____

_____

POW! (Dealing with Aggression) **17**

As we've discussed so far, not only is it possible to slow things down and put your child's experience into words before intervening, doing so can prevent emotions from escalating to the point of total meltdown. But there are exceptions. What if it all happened too quickly to attend to the first signs of their distress or you turn the corner and they are hurting themselves or others? In instances of aggression in particular, getting practical may have to come first to ensure everyone's safety. Sometimes the line is obvious (serious physical fighting) and sometimes it's not (throwing a pillow around the room). Parents have to make their own decision about what's considered serious enough to require immediate action. It can also depend on your child's needs. In some families, throwing a pillow is not okay, but for another family, this may be acceptable because it's a step in the right direction from throwing breakable objects and unlikely to cause serious harm. So how can you still help your child with difficult emotions even in the case of aggressive behavior? Let's go through a scenario to illustrate.

Imagine your 7-year-old grandchild is hitting her 4-year-old brother after he takes her favorite toy.

The Knee-Jerk Response

Much of the time, parents and caregivers will respond with something like:

"Stop hitting him right now!"

"Get away from your brother!"

Sometimes, especially when frustrated, one might forcefully grab the child who is being aggressive, physically remove her from the interaction or space, and punish her.

Imagine for a moment that your child does their version of sibling aggression.

What's your most likely knee-jerk response?

_____

_____

_____

The sequence is different in this situation so that you can deal practically with the situation first. We recommend thinking about it in this order:

Step 1. Getting practical
Step 2. Building a bridge, with emotional translations as needed
Step 3. Putting it into words
Step 4: Getting practical (again)

 ## Step 1. Getting Practical

A child who is using aggression is operating from their more reflexive, automatic "reptile brain." The front part of the brain that helps control impulses and behavior isn't strong enough yet to help her hold back and express herself in a more mature way. This child needs an adult's help to rein herself in and organize her emotional experience. It is an important aspect of connection for caregivers to realize when their child needs help and to provide it.

Practical support: In the preceding scenario, the grandfather can step in here and help the child by doing any of a number of things, such as telling the child to stop, physically separating the children, or redirecting her to another activity. The words he uses to set the limit can also be helpful. Simple words and short sentences are best. For example:

"Sophie, stop hitting Arjan."

Or

"Don't hit. Hitting hurts."

If the child doesn't respond well to words like *stop* or *don't*, You can use alternatives such as:

"Come here, you can hit this pillow."

Taking charge in this situation also supports the child by preventing her from doing more damage that she'll later regret or that might add to a negative image of herself.

 ## Step 2. Building a Bridge

Imagine you're walking in the park and you stop to write an important message on your phone. As you're typing away, someone comes and grabs the phone out of your hand and starts to run away. You want to yell for it back but you're totally overwhelmed and have completely lost your voice! How do you get the thief's attention, call for help, and get your phone back? It probably feels like way too much all at once!

As long as kids have seen the adults around them use nonaggressive strategies, they will use other strategies besides aggression when they can (using their voice, asking an adult for help). But there are many times when the brain short-circuits and children lose their ability to put thoughts into words, especially in younger kids and those with developmental differences (e.g. language delays). Most often this occurs when they feel threatened or overwhelmed with distress. You can think of it as the "fight mode" in the "fight, flight, or freeze" reaction to stress model.

Possible Emotion Translations

Possibility A: "I'm so mad at him for taking my toy and I want him to hurt!"
Possibility B: "I want it back right now!"
Possibility C: "I love my toy, and I'm so upset not to have it I can't stand it!"

Translations for your child:

_____

_____

_____

🗨 Step 3. Putting It into Words

Option 1. "You were so mad at your brother for taking your toy!"

Option 2. "I get why you'd be mad because he wouldn't give it back and nothing you said was working."

Option 3. "You wanted your toy back so badly and you wanted to make him give it to you!"

In your own words:

I can imagine why you'd want to show your brother how mad you are because _____, and because _____, and because _____.

 ## Step 4. Getting Practical (Again)

Once the dust settles, you can continue with practical strategies that go beyond addressing immediate safety issues.

Emotional support: You'll notice that even though the child is behaving in a negative manner, the grandparent isn't suggesting a punishment or criticizing the child. It can be tempting to say something like "What's wrong with you?" or "Stop being so mean to him." The absence of criticism is a step toward emotional support. Over the generations, we've learned that using the old strategy of shaming children when they act out aggressively just doesn't work, and instead can have the opposite effect: When kids believe they are bad, they take on that persona much more readily. If they understand that they are good, but can lose control when they feel bad, they will be much more likely to accept your help to learn strategies to remain in control when big feelings come. You can also use the same strategy of "externalizing the problem" that we mentioned in Chapter 16: "I Hate My Life!"

Practical support: It may be necessary to ensure a cool-down period for everyone before going any further. Instead of time-outs, which used to be widely recommended, we now recommend "time-ins," where you spend some time with the child, helping her settle. This could mean playing a game together or doing some other quiet activity. Parents often worry that this is a "reward" for negative behavior. We see the time with a parent as a way to refill the child's emotional cup and get back on track. Once settled, making amends in some way helps everyone to feel better and provides an opportunity for a valuable lesson to be learned. Simply saying "I'm sorry," especially if an adult is insisting on it, doesn't usually teach the child as much as being asked to think about the other person's perspective and what he would need to feel better. It's very hard for children to consider someone else's perspective when they're angry, and that's one of the reasons it's so helpful for you to attend to the feelings of the child who did the hitting before asking him to think about the child he hit. Some practical ideas for making amends include: making a genuine apology, talking out the original problem, working on a compromise, or offering the injured party something they find meaningful.

Sample Script: POW!

Grandma is making dinner in the kitchen. Nine-year-old Kate loses a game of cards with her sister Emily, who then teases her for being the "loser."

Kate picks up a glass and threatens to throw it across the table at her sister. She has broken things before in a rage.

GRANDMA:	(in a clear and strong voice) "Kate put that glass down now. [getting practical] You have every right to be angry with Emily because she's teasing you. I see that." [putting it into words] (comes a bit closer to Kate)
CHILD:	(angrily puts down the glass on the table) "She's such an idiot!"
GRANDMA:	"I'd be angry too, Kate, because it really hurts when Emily teases you and you don't want her to get away with it. You want her to pay for her teasing." [putting it into words]
CHILD:	Nods. "Isn't she going to get in trouble?"
GRANDMA:	"I can understand why you'd be upset. We don't call each other names in this family, *and* we don't throw things at each other. We need to find a better way. Let's take a few minutes to settle down, and we can talk about it after dinner. Right now, I'd like both of you to help set the table, and we can listen to some music." [getting practical]

Another option to "put it in words" includes validating the child's frustration in a way that redirects their anger toward you – the caregiver – instead. It can be helpful to get children off their current brain track, especially if you aren't currently the "bad guy" in their eyes. This is not so that you can end up *being* the punching bag but so that you can *hold* the punching bag so to speak (that is if you are calm enough yourself). If we look at the example above, Grandma could instead say, "Kate put that glass down. I get why you'd be so angry – especially because I wasn't around to stop her from teasing you." This type of validation highlights what the *caregiver* did or didn't do, rather than focusing on the person (sister) who is the most activating. This can be really effective in the heat of the moment to neutralize the situation.

Common Pitfalls

1. "He's just being a brat." When kids act out, we tend to assume they have more control over their behavior and therefore are being willful or purposefully defiant or threatening. There's no doubt that humans are wired for aggression and that sometimes the child's true intent *is* to harm or hurt another person. Even in these situations, it isn't just a characteristic of the child but a *misguided response* to something. All mammals have the fight or flight response, and many will try to fight when they feel threatened (humans included). It can be hard for parents to recognize the threat because it often isn't a physical threat but an emotional one. Usually, with kids, it's a threat to their self-esteem (like a perceived insult), their belongings or a threat to their perceived safety (like making them do something they're afraid of) that can trigger an aggressive response.

2. "She can't take anything in when she's like that." Some kids can't deal with many words at all when they're angry and out of control. It's another reason why "putting it into words" may need to come later. That being said, it is possible that they are taking in the message even when they seem not to be listening, and so it's a worthwhile practice just in case. To increase the effectiveness of your efforts, when you are using words, try to say them with some energy. Brain science shows that when you can validate your child's really big feelings ("No wonder you're frustrated!") with some energy, even facial expressions and hand gestures, it can help the child calm down even more quickly. It shows them that you understand their distress in a totally different way. The trick is to make sure that your mirroring of their energy is coming from a place of genuinely showing that you get it, *and* that you're not teetering into anger yourself.

3. "When she gets angry, I just lose it." The honest challenge for most of us is that our kids' aggression can be triggering. Their aggression can set off our own alarm bells so intensely that we enter into fight, flight or freeze ourselves. Half the battle is recognizing that we've been triggered and taking a moment to settle as soon as possible. A parent who freezes and tries to act unnaturally calm or who gets really angry in response to their child getting angry can't help the angry child. If you've had a history of traumatic events in your life and your child's aggression triggers those feelings or you notice yourself routinely freezing or fighting back, it can be really helpful to seek out support from a therapist who can help you to disentangle your past from the present (check out Chapter 22: New Directions for ideas that may fit for you).

Reflections

What might make it hard for me to put into words my child's experience in a situation like this?

_____

_____

_____

What might make it hard for me to get practical in a situation like this?

_____

_____

_____

What do I need to deal with this situation like this more confidently in the future?

_____

_____

_____

"Don't Make Me Go to Mom's/Dad's!"   **18**

Ouf. This can be a tricky one. Split families and shared custody can bring all kinds of unique challenges. This scenario is meant for situations where both parents share parenting time and there are no concerns around child protection or safety in either home. We included this scenario because we see it often in our practices, and it causes everyone a lot of distress. It's not uncommon for kids who have a good relationship with both parents to express reluctance to spend time with one or the other, and for a number of reasons we will discuss. Regardless of the issue, it is vital for co-parents to respond to their child's feelings while also supporting their life with the other parent. To do so, we must resist the temptation to take on or even relish in the role of "favorite," even if you see your co-parent as less competent or committed or you don't agree with how they are managing their time with your child.

Scenario: "Don't Make Me Go to Dad's!"

In this scenario, let's imagine that your child is meant to spend the long weekend with her dad, your co-parent. He recently introduced his new partner and they are headed out of town for her family reunion. Your child is already feeling a little uncomfortable about the "girlfriend" situation, let alone going to a reunion with a bunch of people she's never met.

The Knee-Jerk Response

Much of the time, parents and caregivers will respond with something like:

"Let's see what I can sort out to switch weekends."

"You'll be fine. I am sure they'll be other kids your age."

Sometimes, especially when frustrated, one might say:

"That's so soon! Why is your dad doing that to you?!"

Imagine for a moment that your child says to you her version of "Don't make me go to Dad's!"

What's your most likely knee-jerk response?

_____

_____

_____

 # Step 1. Building a Bridge

From the child's perspective, both parents are important, although they may not always feel comfortable expressing that out of loyalty. They may sense conflict between the parents and feel the need to side with one parent or the other. Children usually want to please whoever is right in front of them, and will often hide their own needs to make sure they aren't upsetting their parent. Other children have a hard time with transitioning back and forth between homes. Think of yourself travelling; it's tough to bring clothes and books back and forth, to sleep in a different bed, to possibly be further from friends or school. Sometimes it's as simple as not wanting to do what's on the agenda for the upcoming week or weekend. A child with only one home may not like the family plans, but doesn't have a choice; the child with two homes may feel like it's not fair to be forced to do something when, in her mind, she could just go to her other parent's home instead.

Possible Emotion Translations

Possibility A: "I'm nervous about being in a crowd of people I don't know, and I'm worried Dad won't notice because he'll be paying attention to his girlfriend."

Possibility B: "Transitions are hard no matter what's going on. And most of my stuff is here so that's hard too."

Possibility C: "I'm still heartbroken about your separation, and this week-end will make it feel too real. And what if I like these new people? I don't want to betray you."

Translations for your child:

_____

_____

_____

 ## Step 2. Putting It into Words

Option 1. "I can imagine you might feel a little uneasy about being in a crowd of strangers who all know each other. You might be worried that Dad won't have time to hang out with you."

Option 2. "Transitioning between homes is hard for so many kids, especially since then your stuff is split between two homes too."

Option 3. "Sounds like an out-of-town family reunion wasn't on the list of things you wish you were doing this weekend. In your shoes, I might also be feeling pretty sad, maybe even mad, that Dad and I are moving on with our lives with different people."

In your own words:

I can imagine why you wouldn't want to go to your dad's this weekend because _____, and because _____, and because _____.

 ## Step 3. Getting Practical

Emotional support: Although it may seem counterintuitive, most often, the child needs you to reassure them that their feelings are valid _and_ that you can imagine a scenario where they might actually have some fun with their parent, their new partner, and their family. It might also be helpful to show your child that you are supportive of the cultivation of new relationships. This can be especially relevant if you don't currently have a new partner as your child may worry about you being lonely or jealous. Children who've experienced parental separation can worry that their relationship with each parent may also be fragile or end unexpectedly.

They may need extra reminders, with words and actions, that the parent–child relationship is a different situation and that your bond is too strong to break, no matter how many days or weeks you may be apart at a time.

Practical support: In this scenario, there are several possibilities when it comes to practical needs. One possibility could be to suggest an activity to do together to distract from the anticipatory anxiety, in other words, to help the time go by. If the child's level of unease is more intense, you might work with them to brainstorm strategies to deal with potentially awkward situations. This may include practicing a couple of things to say in the future and encouraging a conversation between the child and your co-parent ahead of time. You might also offer to give your co-parent and his partner a heads up so that they can be "in the know" about your child's feelings and be a part of the solution if the need arises. If you do connect with your co-parent ahead of time, know that they are likely feeling a little anxious too, and so it can wise, kind, and helpful to approach the conversation clearly but also delicately.

Sample Script: "Don't Make Me Go to Mom's!"

CHILD: "Ugh! No! Mom just moved into an apartment in Spring Meadows! With Jamie! Please don't make me go there this weekend!"

PARENT: "Whoa – that's news to me too. Sounds like you're pretty upset about it."

CHILD: "No duh. I'm so embarrassed. I don't want to live in an apartment with them – and especially not across town. I don't want to have to spend the weekend unpacking! All of my friends are going to the mall!"

PARENT: "Okay – makes sense to me. I could imagine why you'd be upset. Sounds like it's a big change, the timing is tricky, and you're not sure yet how you feel about Jamie."

CHILD: "Not sure? No – I'm sure. One hundred percent sure. I hate it."

PARENT: "I don't blame you sweetie. Children want their family together. It's the most normal thing in the world. I can imagine that this move makes it all feel very real. If I were you I'd feel sad, mad, scared – all of the feelings."

CHILD: "It's just going to be *so* complicated. Jamie isn't like you. And Mom gets all weird and lovey when she's around. It's gross."

PARENT: "Yup. I can see how it might be awkward for you to see Mom with someone else. There are going to be a lot of firsts for a while, for all of us. I'm glad that you're talking about it. You know what I think? I think that every person who comes into our family has the potential to make it richer, even if there are some pretty big bumps in the beginning. And even though it's complicated, I am glad your mom has found someone who makes her happy. I've heard Jamie is a pretty cool person. Give her a chance. You might be surprised."

CHILD: "What? Who are you?! You mean – you *want* me to like her?"

PARENT: "It makes sense that you'd be surprised to hear that. I bet it's not always felt that way. You know what – I do. Your family is still evolving, and we don't know yet how it will all unfold. One thing I do know, however, is that your mom loves you deeply, and if she thinks it's time, we've got to trust her decision. Now, it doesn't mean that we can't try to figure out some of the practical details that are overwhelming. What's top on your list?"

CHILD: "Everything! This feels like too much!"

PARENT: "Okay let's break it down. What's the most stressful? Wait – let me put myself in your shoes for a second. Is it that you'll live further away from your school? Or you're worried about having enough privacy or maybe enough alone time with mom? Or the questions from your friends?"

PARENT: "Neither! All of my friends live here!"

CHILD: "In that case, I have an idea. When you come home next week, let's ask one of your friends if they want to come with us, and we'll practice riding the bus from Spring Meadows to here."

*Reminder: The proposed framework is not a magic formula. It can also feel really awkward because it goes against so much of what we were taught about how to respond to children's thoughts and feelings. We do urge you to try it out a few times following the steps as closely as possible as practice really does make a difference over time.

Common Pitfalls

1. "I secretly don't want my child to like my ex's new partner." There's no doubt that one of the most vulnerable moments post-separation is when you hear about or meet the "new partner." If you are like me, I wanted to know everything and anything about them, and nothing at all – at the same time! Talk about bringing up all kinds of old insecurities to the surface. It can also be a really vulnerable thing to have to share your child with other adult caregivers, especially when you don't have choice in the matter. And while these thoughts and feelings may signal that it's time for some extra support from family, friends, or maybe even your therapist, it's also a normal process that takes time to sort out. The key is to be patient with yourself and to find small ways to communicate to your child that you support their relationships with other adult caregivers, until you feel more comfortable with the new reality.

2. "I don't want to support my ex's choices – I don't agree with her decisions." Kids are pretty savvy and will develop their own feelings and opinions about their parents' behavior, especially when things get hard. Usually their conclusions will reflect the upset feelings they feel, in combination with the love that will always be there for both their parents. If you're criticizing your ex to your child with the hope that she will see it your way, it can actually backfire. If children don't get sucked into a loyalty trap, they are more likely to feel the need to defend the parent being criticized and feel bad about the interaction with you. The main thing is that kids feel stressed and caught in the middle if the disagreement involves them, even in small ways. So if providing outright support for your ex's plans is way too much, then maybe you can talk to them directly about the concerns, and out of earshot. If your child is the one expressing concerns about the visit and he is old enough, you can also encourage your child to share his concerns with the other parent. This way, you are supporting your child to develop healthy communication strategies. If you suspect it will be difficult for your child's voice to be heard and your relationship with your co-parent is too conflictual, a therapist can help your family to develop healthier ways of sorting through these types of difficulties.

3. "Too late. I already fell into the trap. What do I do now?" You and thousands of others! Divorce is a relatively new phenomenon in our society and goodness knows, just like there's no handbook for parenting, there's certainly no handbook for navigating the intricacies of family reconstruction. The good news is that it's never too late. You can start off as simply as "Kiddo, I realized that I made a mistake when I criticized your mom" and take it from there. Kids so appreciate it when we show up as normal, flawed human beings, and however the conversation goes, you now have a framework to respond to their feelings. For more on this style of responding, check out the next chapter: The "Do-Over".

Reflections

What might make it hard for me to put into words my child's experience in a situation like this?

_____

_____

_____

What might make it hard for me to get practical in a situation like this?

_____

_____

_____

What do I need to deal with a situation like this more confidently in the future?

_____

_____

_____

The "Do-Over"　　　　　**19**

Maybe you've had a conversation with your child about school or home-work and you realize you missed an opportunity to connect with them using this new style of communication. Or maybe, it's a scenario where things really fell apart and you're both fed up and exhausted. You know, the situation where you're left feeling awful, maybe even with a shame-hangover for things you said or did? For me, it's like a sinking pit. In the moment, it can feel bad or like there's been irreparable damage or that you're doomed to repeat the cycle forevermore. Although things even-tually calm down and smooth over, it can still feel awkward and unfin-ished, and the regret for not having handled things more calmly and productively can linger.

Whether a minor slip or a major miss, one of the most liberating things we've learned is that it's always possible to have a "do-over" in parenting. That is an opportunity to replay the scene – with much less of a charge – and with more conscious participation. Not only that, the do-over can actually strengthen the adult–child relationship even more than man-aging every situation smoothly the first time around. Not that we want to screw up on purpose, but the process of missing the mark with your child's emotions and then going back to repair the rupture really does build resilience and trust. Thank goodness! You see, it's really true that we are not striving for perfection here. In other words, it's not what happens, it's what happens next!

Scenario: The "Do-Over"

Your 10-year-old is yelling at his 7-year-old brother – again. You've been alone with both kids all weekend and have had to separate them multiple times for fighting. This time, it's over a video game controller. You've had enough. Your interaction with Kyle goes something like this:

PARENT: "Kyle, I've had enough of you! You're 10 years old! You know better, and you're acting like a jerk. Get up to your room!"
CHILD: "You can't make me!"
PARENT: "That's it! Get up to your room or you're not going to that birthday party!"
CHILD: "I hate you." (sulks away)
PARENT: "I really don't care right now!"

 ## Step 1. Rebuilding the Bridge

The child in this scenario is upset twice over. The first time, he was upset by something to do with his brother and the game controller, but the second time was with the interaction with his parent. We would argue that it's the second upset that needs to be dealt with first. The 10-year-old here will feel hurt that his mom sees him in a negative light and is saying she's had enough of him and that she doesn't care that he hates her. He may understand that's it just something said in anger and frustration in the moment, but it's also possible he may not. As we've mentioned, kids just don't have the same ability for complex thought required to appreciate the bigger picture. That's why sometimes they can come to believe that their parent sees them as "bad" or worse, doesn't love them. Nothing else is likely to go in until the hurt with the parent is addressed. Why? Because the parent is the guide, and when you've had a falling out with your guide, you care less about the path toward "Calm Child Who Behaves Maturely". It's also because your child is most wired to you, and at that age, when things fall apart between you, it can be the most destabilizing.

To that last point, no matter how defiant, angry, and uncaring kids act, they care deeply about how we see them. This may be hard to believe when they send multiple messages to the contrary or when they come at us toe-to-toe. Kids may act big and tough, but compared with us they are small and vulnerable in that, at the most basic level, they depend on us for their survival.

Even though we can't fully take back what we say, it can be so powerful to go back and address what happened. For so many reasons! First, when you go back and work through the feelings related to a challenging interaction – even if years later, the memory of the interaction gets moved from the brain's long-term storage "I'll never forget what my parent once said to me" cabinet to the one that stores the more mundane memories categorized in the "things that happened in the past" cabinet. In scientific terms, memories are made up of different parts. The emotional tags of memories are found in cells of the *limbic system* and in particular, the *amygdala*. Research has shown that these emotional memory "tags" can be modified after the fact in that when they are targeted and processed, that particularly memory loses its super-charge. In fact, if you're lucky, the do-over can upgrade the memory of the event to the highly coveted "times when my parents modeled the value of taking responsibility when mistakes are made" cabinet or better yet, the "even more proof my parents really care about me and our relationship" cabinet.

 ## Step 2. Putting It into Words

After the 10-year-old sulks up to his room and the 7-year-old is content playing video games, the parent finally has a few minutes to herself to catch her breath. She realizes she spoke harshly to her son and wants to make it right. She thinks about ways to start the "do-over." She decides to give herself a few more minutes to breathe her way back to earth and then goes up to her son's bedroom to apologize and give examples of what could have been said or done instead:

Option 1. "Hey, bud. I'm really sorry for how I talked to you before. It really wasn't fair. No kidding you were mad at me, and probably even more so after I said I didn't care that you hated me in that moment. I could imagine that part really stung because I'm your mom and I'm supposed to see the good in you, even when things get out of hand. **What I should have done** was help you to calm down and solve the problem."

Option 2. "Kyle, you have every right to be upset. I'm sorry I said I'd had enough of you. It wasn't okay for me to say that. I should have stayed calmer or found another to say that I was frustrated. **What I should have said** was 'Kyle, I'm really struggling to keep my cool right now. I want to help you but I'm going to need a minute. Turn off the console, and we'll all sit down to figure this out in a little while.'"

Option 3. Slips a note under Kyle's door that says:

> Dear Kyle, I am really sorry for what I said. I imagine that really hurt.
> I got really upset, and I should have found another way to handle
> the situation. **What I should have done** was listen to your frustra-
> tion and offered you some support to figure out the problem. I care
> a lot about your feelings and our relationship. I will do my best to
> remember the steps from that parenting book the next time. ☺

In your own words:

I'm sorry for what I said because _____, and because _____,
and because _____. What I should have said/done was _____.

 ## 3. Getting Practical

Emotional support: Reconnection is primary here. When we say something insulting or hurtful to someone we love, it temporarily shakes their
trust in us as someone who is emotionally safe. Acknowledging the hurt
followed by a clear description of what else could have been said or
done helps to rebuild trust – and quickly. It also helps to keep children
from blaming themselves or others (depending on how they are wired)
or thinking they "deserve" to be put down. The other important needs
here are to feel loved, valued, and respected by one's primary caregivers.
When a parent or caregiver can apologize and try again or offer an alternative, it sends the message to the child that "you are important to me." A
hug or some other show of love and softness will help ease the situation
once the child is ready.

Practical support: Once the storm blows over and you and your child
are back to baseline or close to it, you can talk about the next time. For
example, I have asked my kids to let me know when I'm falling off the
tracks. Although it's not their responsibility to regulate us, when you can
agree beforehand on a sentence or a code word, it can help prevent a
blastoff. It also gives your child a feeling of control in a moment when it
feels like the relationship is in a tough spot. In the meantime, it's also our
job to work toward a change to reduce the likelihood of a recurrence.

Okay – those are some points to ponder for the first part of the "do-
over." The first incident is still unresolved in this scenario, and so now it's
time to address the initial issue of the fight over the controller.

The parent here can now *put into words* her understanding of her child's initial distress with something like "And no wonder you were upset with your brother because …":

Option 1: "You've been trying to play your game all afternoon, and he keeps wanting you to play with him."

Option 2: "I could imagine it's getting on your nerves because I bet you'd rather play alone."

Option 3: "It might feel like he's doing it on purpose, and you want your turn with the good controller."

 ## Getting Practical

Emotional support: As in the aftermath of all child misbehavior, one of the primary needs for the child is your continued love and acceptance – similar to Chapter 11: "I'm so Bad/Stupid …" Then, engaging your child in a conversation in what happened for him can help him to clarify the layers of his experience, therefore helping him get closer to finding words to handle the situation next time rather than fighting. Depending on your child's age and personality, you might also give them some space to let them cool down. Doing so can also convey that it's okay for them to be upset with you. Do remember, however, that "giving space" looks different for different kids and a plan for reconnection is always important to communicate.

Practical support: Now it's possible to go back and problem-solve around the sibling fight and find a compromise or solution. Depending on the severity of the conflict, it may also be necessary to separate the brothers, or to increase supervision for a while, or to structure some other kind of family activity where fighting is less likely. It is equally important to look at what you need as a parent to get through the rest of the day. Finally, when kids repeatedly act out, it can be also be a sign that their parent needs more support, and so it can be really helpful to focus on yourself to see what kind of help you might benefit from in order to get through this tough phase.

The beauty of the "do-over" lies in the fact that when you go back and put into words the child's initial hurt and then offer support, it can still have the same effect as if you'd done it in the moment. It may even be more effective because the child is a lot calmer than he was before.

In fact, we've witnessed ourselves (and heard from other parents too) that when this happens, children are more likely to then try to right their own wrong – either with you or their sibling in this example – and often without prompting. It can lead to a pretty cool domino effect.

*Reminder: Your ace in the hole is sincerity. Thanks to their mirror neurons, your child's brain will register that your efforts are genuine, leading to a release of calming neurochemicals regardless of how well you follow the exact structure provided.

Sample Script: The "Do-Over"

PARENT: "Kyle, I've had enough of you! You're 10 years old! You know better, and you're acting like a jerk. Get up to your room!"

CHILD: "You can't make me!"

PARENT: "That's it! Get up to your room, or you're not going to that birthday party! You're driving me crazy!"

CHILD: "I hate you." (sulking away)

PARENT: "I really don't care right now!"

PARENT: (an hour later) "Hey bud. I'm really sorry for how I talked to you before. I don't blame you for saying that you hate me, because what I said really wasn't nice. And it wasn't fair to say that I didn't care. That must have made it feel even worse. I should have found a way to calm down before reacting."

CHILD: "Mom – you called me a jerk."

PARENT: "Yeah and I really shouldn't have said that. You're not a jerk; you're a frustrated kid who's had to deal with too many arguments with his brother. Sometimes moms and dads get angry and say or do something hurtful too. We all need to learn to treat each other well even when we're super frustrated. Next time I lose my cool, you have my permission to say: Mom – you're not acting like an adult! How about that?"

CHILD: (smiles) "Sure, but now *you* should get grounded from your phone!"

PARENT: "Good one. Okay – now back to what got this going in the first place. When I saw how upset you were, what I could have said was: No kidding you're mad! It's hard to deal with little brothers, and sometimes it feels like you can't do anything else to make it stop."

CHILD: "Exactly! It's like you always take his side."

PARENT: "I get it. Sometimes I see you as the big guy and him as the little guy, and I forget you're both still kids. I get how much that must hurt, because you're my little guy too. I do know he has a part to play in the fights. It sounds like we may also need to sit down and figure out a system for those controllers. Let's give it a bit more time and go to the pool together before dinner to change things up."

CHILD: "Okay."

PARENT: "Good. But first, I have to find your brother because he probably has hurt feelings too. You might also want to say something to him. What do you think?"

CHILD: "Yeah, I will. I'll apologize in the car on the way to the pool."

PARENT: "Good idea." (leans in for a hug)

Common Pitfalls

1. "I shouldn't have to apologize to my child." It's not the first time we suggest an apology. An apology can be a meaningful component of the "do-over." However, if you were raised by a parent who didn't apologize or admit to mistakes (it was a cultural thing for a looong time), then this whole idea may feel foreign. It can feel like it's messing with the right hierarchy where the parent is in charge. Some people think apologies show weakness, but in relationships, they usually show strength. An apology from parent to child doesn't mean parents are blaming themselves or focusing on their own "mistake" – it's actually a *deep validation* or acknowledgment of the fact that the conversation or interaction didn't go well. It shows the parent has self-awareness. It's *because* the parent is in charge that she is also most responsible for the emotional climate between parent and child and can model taking responsibility for losing their temper. Kids will learn that they, too, can have "do-overs" in relationships when their parents show them how to admit mistakes or address conflict constructively. If an apology still feels too vulnerable, then you can circle back to address the missed opportunity for validation using this sentence starter: "Remember when X happened, and I said Y? What I should have said was Z."

2. "What if she doesn't forgive me?" Many kids will act like a turtle when hurt and retreat into their shells. They may need time to be open to your attempts to repair the rupture. Rest assured, however, that even when the child is silent, they can still hear and take in your words. If you can wait through this (and not interpret it as defiance or rejection), it will pay off. Children desperately want to make up after arguments with their parents. They need you, depend on you, want to please, and the pit they feel inside after a meltdown may be even bigger than the one you feel. They may deny this to save face and not let you see they're hurt, but it's likely there. Few kids won't soften after a parent makes a genuine attempt at a "do-over." Even those kids who stay quiet or shut you out will eventually come around in time. If the silence persists, you can go back to Chapter 10: "I'm Not Talking to You …" for inspiration.

3. "My partner in caregiving always blows up then apologizes. I don't think that's good enough." This is an important point. Apologizing and showing we understand our child's hurt isn't enough if we keep repeating the same hurtful behaviors. We all get "do-overs." However, if we find ourselves needing them multiple times a week, it is likely a sign that there's too much stress on the family system and more support is needed. It may be that co-parenting tensions are feeding into the problem or it's a matter of everyone being exhausted with the stressors of life. It may even be one's own mental health issues creeping in. Whatever the case, caregivers needs to find a different answer if the same thing keeps happening. A partner in caregiving may get very defensive if you try to point this out, and so we strongly encourage the use of this framework to get the message across in a way that is loving and productive (for more on this topic, check out Chapter 20: "You're too Soft! and You're too Hard!"). You may even choose to enlist the support of a therapist to get help to bring up your concerns about your partner's struggles since your own unresolved feelings might also be tangled in the web of the family's pain (see Chapter 22: New Directions for more information regarding possible avenues for support).

A situation from the past where I could practice a "do-over":

_____

_____

_____

What might make it hard for me to initiate a "do-over"?

_____

_____

_____

What do I need to make it more likely that I will try a "do-over"?

_____

_____

_____

"You're too Soft!" and "You're too Hard!" **20**

This chapter is a little different. Instead of focusing on statements commonly made by kids, this one tackles exchanges that are all too common between parents or between any two caregivers for the same child (for example, mom and grandma, parent and stepparent, or between exes). In every co-parenting relationship, both parties come with their own set of values, beliefs, and tendencies. Our unique parenting style is most influenced by the way we were raised – either we adopted a learned pattern of behavior, or we developed a style in reaction to what we experienced or a little of both. We've also seen over the years that when it comes to parenting, the adage "opposites attract" is perhaps more common than "birds of a feather flock together." This means that you may often find yourself at loggerheads with your partner in caregiving at exactly the time when you most want their support.

It's also very rare that co-parents always agree on discipline and childrearing. When kids are struggling, it's even less common. More often than not, they get polarized into two camps: "too soft" and "too hard." For example, when one parent is softer in their approach to parenting and the other is tougher, there is a risk that both parents end up polarizing in their tendencies. For example, if I am softer, and I see you as too tough, I will become softer still, to compensate for your toughness. When you see me get even softer, that has the potential to make you even tougher, again to compensate for my softness. This cycle can go on and on to the point where the kids are being cared for in the "extremes" and the conflict between you is so high, you can hardly address each other, let alone identify the problem that got it going in the first place. Sometimes, just knowing about this phenomenon is enough for both parents to come a little ways towards the middle. Other times, it can be useful to be more active in interrupting the cycle using the framework we've been working with throughout the book.

But first – warning! It's definitely more challenging to use this way of relating to your partner in caregiving. That said, it can be just as effective. The same principles apply with respect to the power of validation and support on the brain no matter with whom you're talking. Remember: When the external environment (you) can speak the internal experience of the other (your partner), their brain's alarm bells will reduce in intensity – whether the alarm is ringing because of your child's meltdown or the start or a disagreement with you. In other words, your partner will be calmer, more flexible, and more reasonable, and you might feel like you are on the same page (despite perhaps being on different lines of that page).

Scenario A: "You're too Soft!"

In this scenario, let's assume it's your child's bedtime, and she's had a hard day at school. She is begging you to stay up just a little later. You agree to 15 more minutes. Later on, when your child is in bed, she yells down to you for a glass of water. You get up from the couch and hear your co-parent mutter under her breath: "You are too soft!"

The Knee-Jerk Response

Much of the time, partners in caregiving will respond with something like:

"Please don't. Your criticism isn't helpful."

"I'm exhausted, and I just want bedtime to be over."

Sometimes, especially when frustrated, one might say:

"Yeah, well, you're too tough. It would be nice for all of us if you were a little softer once in a while."

Imagine for a moment that your partner in caregiving says to you her version of: "You're too soft!"

What's your most likely knee-jerk response?

_____

_____

_____

Step 1. Building a Bridge

If your co-parent complains about you "being too soft," it is likely that they really value qualities such as independence and resilience. In fact, it may be one of the reasons why you were attracted to this person in the first place! Across many cultures around the world these values are held in high regard. Why? Well, some argue that after World War II, a military mentality seeped into the realm of parenting. As such, it is not unusual for our parents (and theirs) to have instilled in us the need to be mentally and physically tough. Another reason some parents want to ensure their child is independent as soon as possible is out of fear and love. Fear that as young adults, they won't make it on their own or that they will be more vulnerable when faced with challenges. Some parents are also keenly aware that they won't be around forever and so – from a place of love – they do their best to prepare their child with as many practical skills to ensure their child is successful *and* that they are well equipped to navigate life's ups and downs with relative ease. We've observed that when a child is affected by a physical, cognitive, or emotional challenge, this drive can become even stronger.

There's another possibility we'd like to propose in the context of couples. Is it possible that when your partner complains that you're too soft with the kids, he may be yearning for some of that softness or caretaking himself? This may not apply to all readers who can relate with this scenario but under the surface of the criticism and complaint can lie a vulnerable longing for a little extra TLC. Similarly, when your partner sees you getting up again – especially if he knows you're tired – he may be concerned for you, especially if he feels like you're less emotionally available in the relationship when you are burnt out. Consider the possibility …

Possible Emotion Translations

Possibility A: "I'm worried that if you are always too accommodating, our child won't learn to survive without us."

Possibility B: "I'm worried you'll burn yourself out if you're always catering to so many of the demands our child makes."

Possibility C: "I miss you. Our time together is always cut short by the children's needs, so it hurts when it seems like more precious time is slipping away."

Translations for your partner in caregiving:

_____

_____

_____

*Reminder: First, try to guess the context: Did something just happen recently? Does your co-parent have a pattern of getting upset in similar situations? The key is to ask yourself: What is the most vulnerable explanation for their complaint?

 ## Step 2. Putting It into Words

Option 1. "I can understand why you'd object – it might seem like she's got me wrapped around her little finger and that would be a problem."

Option 2. "I can see how you might be worried that now she'll try to get more time every night and that bedtime will become even more of a challenge."

Option 3. "It must be frustrating when it looks like I'm choosing to do more for her and sacrificing some of the precious little time we have together."

In your own words:

I can imagine why you would think I was too soft because _____, and because _____, and because _____.

 ## Step 3. Getting Practical

Emotional support: In this scenario, although it may not seem like it on the surface, the co-parent's need is usually in the domain of comfort and reassurance. This can be surprising because the delivery can feel a little prickly. Since we know that "fighting back" only sets you up for a duel – and a much less pleasant evening – we strongly recommend that you look beyond the surface and offer your partner in caregiving the emotional support for the vulnerable need that lies beneath the prickles. If it feels genuine, you can say something like, "I can assure you honey, I want this kid to become independent as much as you do!" or "Don't leave that spot, I'll be there as soon as I can. I really want to hang out with you tonight." Your co-parent also wants to know that you don't think she is a meanie. There can be shame in feeling like the "bad guy"; co-parents want acceptance from each other, a belief in their positive intentions, and respect for the unique gifts they bring to the family.

Practical support: First, an exhausted parent is inevitably less flexible and less able to stick to limits. In this case, the practical need may be sleep or just a break. Second, co-parents are often too tired to nurture their own relationship. When kids are having a tough time, it leaves even less time for the adults. Yet we know that kids thrive when their parents are doing well, and so just from the point of view of helping kids emotionally, devoting time to the co-parent relationship is a sound investment. You may even get more "bang for your buck" focusing more on the relationship between caregiving partners than the parent–child relationship in some circumstances. So when factoring in the pros and cons of any parenting decisions, like a firmer bedtime routine, your own well-being and the health of the co-parent and/or couple relationship do come into play.

Sample Script A: "You're too Soft!"

PARENT 1:   Getting up to make their 12-year-old son toast: "Do you want butter or peanut butter?"

PARENT 2:   (mumbling under breath) "Really?"

Later, when the children are off to school:

PARENT 2:   "You are way too accommodating. He's old enough to get his own toast."

PARENT 1:   "Yes he is. I can imagine when you see me cater to him like this, that you might worry that he's going to become spoiled."

PARENT 2:   "He's already too spoiled."

PARENT 1:   "We do give him way more than what we got as kids that's for sure. And it makes sense to me that you'd want him to grow up to be a responsible, self-sufficient adult."

PARENT 2:   "I do. Don't you?"

PARENT 1:   "I do too. For many reasons, including that we'll have more time together when that time comes. And I don't blame you for being worried about the kids and their capacity to be independent. It's such an important life skill; we won't be around forever, so they need to figure it out. I want you to know that we do want the same thing, and I am committed to getting there. I'll tell you what – I'll recruit those little gremlins to help me with dinner and clean up. And it's time we line up a babysitter for a date night."

Common Pitfalls

1. "His parents weren't very patient with him, so he doesn't know any better." It may be true that the person with the "harder" stance was raised in a more authoritarian home or got less comfort as a child. It may even be true that he doesn't have a good sense of developmental norms. Don't get us wrong, it's really great to have compassion and understanding about the reasons why your partner in caregiving has adopted certain parenting patterns. However, if you don't address your concerns, you are more likely to get stuck in the pattern of overcompensation. Each parent will bring their own values to the situation, and it is more helpful to start from a place of respecting *and* addressing differences of opinion.

2. "You don't know my ex/partner. He/she is just difficult." On the flip side, it can be very easy to see the worst in a co-parent when we disagree on issues in parenting (guilty!), especially when we are doing our very best or when we feel like we are carrying more of the load. However, as soon as one parent feels his or her opinion is devalued, it will be hard to stay calm enough to have a productive conversation or learn more about how you see things or what else might be helpful in the moment. Just like with kids, validating someone doesn't mean agreeing. It's all about temporarily taking their perspective to help their brain to calm. People of all ages respond to validation in this way and because increased calm equals increased flexibility, they are then more open to perspective taking, feedback, and creative problem-solving. Parenting is hard, and feeling supported is half the battle. Sometimes we need to be the first domino to create the mindset that is necessary to get things moving in a better direction for all involved.

Reflections

What might make it hard for me to put into words my co-parent's experience in a situation like this?

_____

_____

_____

What might make it hard for me to get practical in a situation like this?

_____

_____

_____

What do I need to deal with a situation like this more confidently in the future?

_____

_____

_____

Guidelines for Co-Parents in Times of Stress

Whatever is going on between you, it can be helpful to agree on a set of guidelines to follow in the heat of the moment. Here are some suggestions:

1. It can be helpful to acknowledge that arguing between co-parents only makes things worse for the child and harder for each parent to act calmly and decisively.
2. It's generally better for only one parent to manage an upset child at a time.
3. The other parent can jump in when asked for help or if there is danger of physical or emotional harm.
4. When help is requested, it is useful to be specific. Do you want emotional support, backup that the co-parent is on the same page, or for the co-parent to take over?

5. The definition of serious emotional harm may need to be discussed and agreed upon. Kids and relationships are resilient and most arguments cause no lasting harm, but it is good to have a plan in place if things start to get out of control.
6. Each parent will learn more quickly when allowed to sort things out with the child without the other co-parent jumping in.
7. It you feel a need to intervene that can't wait, you can step away from the situation briefly to offer your co-parent emotional support or commiseration and share any concerns that you may have (just remember to avoid criticism as a strategy to course-correct).
8. Make time to debrief afterward. This makes it easier to save any concerns or requests until after the child has settled. Then you can plan for next time.

If, for whatever reason, one or both of you get total amnesia about any or all of this and you erupt in front of the kids (this will be an issue of when, not if!), then we remind you that the "do-over" can be a powerful practice between co-parents and with the child/ren. Although we aim to protect kids from our conflicts as much as possible, it is true that what happens next can be what's most influential.

Scenario B: "You're too Hard!"

Okay – flip side of the coin! Say your 6-year-old lies about breaking your favorite mug. You love that mug, but you value honesty even more. And this isn't the first time; he's lied about not brushing his teeth, sneaking screen time and having no reading homework. You think age 6 is plenty old enough to know right from wrong and to learn the consequences of lying to your parents. Once you find out the real story behind your shattered mug, you say to him:

> Joey, it's not okay to lie, and you need to be more careful. I've told you this before. I'm taking away your building set for 2 weeks, and you need to do some chores to pay me back for the mug.

You see your partner eyeing the conversation. Later that night, after Joey's in bed, he comes to you and says: "You were way too hard on Joey today. He's only 6!"

The Knee-Jerk Response

Much of the time, partners in caregiving will respond with something like:

"Yes, but he has to learn his lesson somehow!"

"I don't think we're doing him any favors by handling it this way."

Sometimes, especially when frustrated, one might say:

"Maybe if you didn't let him walk all over you, he wouldn't try to pull the wool over our eyes."

Imagine for a moment that your partner in caregiving says to you his or her version of "You're too hard!"

What's your most likely knee-jerk response?

_____

_____

_____

*Reminder: If you are feeling stressed, upset, or overwhelmed, engaging in this mental exercise can be a real challenge. You might find that taking a break or a couple of deep breaths might make it easier to brainstorm possible emotional translations.

 ## Step 1. Building a Bridge

Part of our role as parents and caregivers is to ensure that kids grow up to be competent and productive members of society. Another part is to protect them for harm and support them to develop a healthy identity. It's important to believe that your co-parent truly does want the best for your child. Even if sometimes they behave in ways you don't like (or often behave in ways you don't like), underneath it is almost always a desire to teach the child something helpful or protect what she believes to be the child's best interests. Just like the parent whose tough stance is fueled by fear, so is the parent who tends toward softness. The parent who criticizes you for being "too hard" is likely afraid that the child will be pushed beyond what he can cope with at his age. They may be concerned that the child will be harmed emotionally or that your approach will damage your relationship with them. Their instinct will be to protect the child and protect your relationship with the child, even if in ways that don't feel so supportive.

Possible Emotion Translations

Possibility A: "I'm worried our kid will feel so overwhelmed by the punishment that he misses the point."

Possibility B: "I'm worried he will resent you for being too tough or grow distant from you and that could lead to even more acting out."

Possibility C: "I'm worried he won't be able to cope without his building set for all that time and I'll end up being the one to deal with it since I'm home more often."

Translations for your partner in caregiving:

_____

_____

_____

*Reminder: The idea here is to connect with their good intentions, vulnerable feelings, or need for connection driving their current state of being, even if on the surface it doesn't seem so.

 ## Step 2. Putting It into Words

Option 1. "I get why you'd think I'm too hard on him. He's a little guy, and you don't want him to get overwhelmed, shut down, or act out even more."

Option 2. "Sounds like you're worried he's going to take it personally and feel worse about himself."

Option 3. "I see that it bothers you, and that makes sense to me. I know how much you want Joey and I to have a good relationship, and you worry that he'll get distant or shut down."

In your own words:

I can imagine why you would think I was too hard on him because
_____, and because _____, and because _____.

 ## Step 3. Getting Practical

Emotional support: The parent who says, "you're too hard" usually
wants to protect your child from too much distress or low self-worth.
Therefore, the emotional need is conveying to them – genuinely and
convincingly – that you would never want to cause harm to your child.
They also want to know that you are making a rational decision and not
one fueled by anger or vengeance. Perhaps most important, they want
to know that you also value and are committed to maintaining, even fos-
tering closeness and connection with your child, despite your inclination
for a tougher stance.

Practical support: Once you've provided your partner in caregiving
with emotional support, it can be helpful to listen to his or her point of
view about discipline and discuss your differences of opinion when you
are both calm. Chances are really good that you want similar things, but
have different ways of achieving those goals. You may create a plan to
communicate love and connection to your child during or after conflict,
including when setting limits. It also helps to set limits that you can personally enforce so that your co-parent doesn't feel burdened by having
to set limits which they didn't particularly endorse.

Sample Script B: "You're too Hard!"

PARENT 1: "Honey, Leo broke his tablet last night. He asked me if we
could help him to pay for the repair. What do you think?"

PARENT 2: "No chance. That tablet is his responsibility, and so getting
it fixed is his concern. He shouldn't have been so careless."

PARENT 1: "Seriously? He's only 12 years old!"

PARENT 2: "Okay ... I'm taking it you think I'm being too hard on him?"

PARENT 1: "Well, yeah! How's he supposed to make enough money to
pay for that? He's had such a rough go the past few weeks.
He needs to spend time on homework."

PARENT 2:	"Ah – I'm guessing you don't want to make his life unnecessarily hard, especially since school has been getting him down. I could imagine that you'd be worried that he'll lose it if we don't help him to catch a break."
PARENT 1:	"I *am* worried that he'll get even more stressed and refuse to do his homework and I don't want to go there again."
PARENT 2:	"I see where you are coming from, especially since you're doing more of the heavy-lifting with school. Okay, well I know it would make life easier in the short-term to just replace the screen, but I think he'll feel better and more competent in the long run if he can pay for the fix himself. I can assure you, I'm not just trying to be a jerk. Sounds like I should also check in with him a bit more often to see how he's doing. And don't worry – I'll be patient with him."
PARENT 1:	"Fine. But we need to help him figure out some realistic ways to earn money if he gets overwhelmed."
PARENT 2:	"That's fair. Okay – when do you think is the best time to break the news?"

Common Pitfalls

1. "He's disrespecting me when he questions my parenting." You may feel annoyed, disrespected, criticized, and/or judged by your co-parent when she accuses you of being too tough on your kid. You need to honor those feelings. They are legitimate. However, any of the knee-jerk reactions we described will usually lead down a spiral of blaming each other and miss the point of figuring out what to do to help your child. Your co-parent's reaction may feel like she doesn't trust or respect you, but it is actually much less about you and more about her fear of your child feeling too much pain. Parents will do anything to prevent harm to their child; it's the most basic instinct, and while your intentions are good, your firmer stance can set off alarm bells for your co-parent so that she jumps in to protect the child from perceived emotional harm. It still doesn't feel good that your co-parent might see your interaction this way, but it is better to understand that it's her fear at play. You can also let your co-parent know you feel badly when she jumps in, and that will diffuse the situation far more than fighting back.

2. "I hate always having to be the 'bad guy.'" It can be endlessly frustrating for the stricter parent to be the one who consistently has to set the limits. It's enough to have the child push against them, but even worse if you feel like your partner in caregiving contradicts you. It doesn't feel good, and it also makes it harder to manage the child's behavior. It can feel like, "if only my co-parent just toughened up, everything would be better." As we explained earlier, the more you try to suggest she parent more like you or you defend your firmness, the more anxious she will get. Showing that you get her perspective will lower her anxiety, decrease her need to "balance things out" or "protect," and put her in a better position to maintain firmer limits. It's also possible that, on the flip side, your partner does more of the heavy lifting with the emotions or perhaps she is the family's "manager." Consider that as a team, you are better together, and it will make it easier to play off each other's strengths and weaknesses as you sort out a more balanced approach to collaborative parenting.

Reflections

What might make it hard for me to put into words my co-parent's experience in a situation like this?

_____

_____

_____

What might make it hard for me to get practical in a situation like this?

_____

_____

_____

What do I need to deal with a situation like this more confidently in the future?

_____

_____

_____

Figure 20.1 Knee-jerk response

Figure 20.2 Validation and support

"Why Are You Talking to Me Like That?" 21

We saved the best for last! Over the years, some parents have shared with us that their child (or co-parent) initially responded to their efforts to implement these communication and support strategies with surprise, suspicion, and even full-on rejection. Others were worried about how to navigate such a response, making it so they were less likely to try out the approach. If the manner of relating to your loved ones outlined in this book is really different from your norm, you can probably bet someone in your family will react when you first try it out. Families tend to behave in predictable patterns; when someone breaks the mold, the reaction is to be expected and doesn't mean what you're doing is wrong or unhelpful. You can be guided by the ideas in this chapter regardless of how your loved one responds, and it can sometimes take more than one "round" of doing so for your loved one to settle. At first it can feel a bit like "whack-a-mole" where a new reaction pops up as soon as you validated the last one, except that with this version every player is a winner ... eventually!

Scenario A: "Why Are You Talking to Me Like That?"

In this scenario, let's assume a stepmom used the framework as described in the book to respond to her stepchild's refusal to cooperate. She validates the child's resistance, offers support, and then the kid looks at her incredulously and exclaims, "Why are you talking to me like that?"

The Knee-Jerk Response

Much of the time, parents and caregivers will respond with something like:

"Hey – It's supposed to feel better when I talk like that!"

"Never mind, I guess it doesn't work."

Sometimes, especially when frustrated, one might say:

"Well forget that. I won't even try to understand your feelings anymore."

Imagine for a moment that your child says to you her version of "Why are you talking to me like that?"

What's your most likely knee-jerk response?

_____

_____

_____

 Step 1. Building a Bridge

This bridge is easily built with a look back at our own childhood. Can you imagine if your parent came home one day and, instead of getting defensive or shrinking in the face of your resistance or anger, they validated it! Or when you dared tell your teacher you didn't feel like more homework, she could understand your point of view (even if she still assigned you those dang verb tenses!). Given that most of us were raised during a time when resistance and anger were considered "bad," and parents and other adult influencers were strongly advised to maintain an authoritarian stance, it makes sense that we'd find it totally bizarre if they suddenly responded this way. Even though parenting trends have shifted in a generally "softer" direction, validation and "being with" difficult feelings is still not the norm. Not just with anger, with other feelings too (refer back to the various knee-jerk responses in Chapter 3: Potential Roadblocks – they come from somewhere!)

Possible Emotion Translations

Possibility A: "I'm surprised by your response because it's so different from what I'm used to."

Possibility B: "I'm not sure I trust the sincerity of your words. It feels like you're trying to trick me into feeling better or doing something you want me to do."

Possibility C: "I'm worried this is a temporary change, and I'd better not get too used to it."

Translations for your child:

_____

_____

_____

⬭ Step 2. Putting It into Words

Option 1. "I don't blame you for reacting this way – it's really different from what usually comes out of my mouth."

Option 2. "I can imagine you might be suspicious, like maybe I'm trying to make fun of you or trick you."

Option 3. "It's got to be confusing that I'm not talking like I usually do. You might wonder if I really mean what I'm saying."

In your own words:

I can imagine why you would react this way because _____, and because _____, and because _____.

*Reminder: The idea here is to connect with your child's good intentions, vulnerable feelings, or need for connection driving their reaction, if on the surface it doesn't seem so.

Step 3. Getting Practical

Emotional support: Meeting the emotional need in this context can be a really awesome opportunity to deepen your relationship with your loved one, whether it's your child or your partner reacting to your new style of communication. In this instance, you can acknowledge that, yes they are in fact picking up on a new style, and that it might be a bit choppy or feel unnatural for a while as you try it out. You can follow that up with a commitment to increase the frequency with which you connect on a more emotional level when things are stressful or hard between you. One parent shared that she simply told her child that: "This is going to be our new normal, and I am going to keep working at it so that our family can grow even stronger together. Even if it feels awkward at first!"

Practical support: Once your loved one can feel that your intentions are genuine, you can invite him to give you feedback on your style. For example, as we mentioned earlier in the book, some older kids who are trying to sort out who they are as individuals might prefer you to use the phrase "I imagine you'd feel" versus "I can understand," because it helps them to feel like the separate individuals they are truly becoming; or better yet, "When I put myself in your shoes, I can imagine that from your point of view, you might feel _____." Kids who are already competent at figuring out their own feelings might feel like it's overstepping for you to make an assumption. Other kids are happy for you to "understand" how they feel or to help them figure it out. It makes them feel heard and seen. In some cases, we just won't know which style fits best until it happens and the other person reacts. That's all part of the process.

Sample Script: "Why Are You Talking to Me Like That?"

PARENT: "... And so it makes sense to me that you'd feel worried or even upset about the change in plans."

CHILD: "Huh? Are you being serious?"

PARENT: "What do you mean, love?"

CHILD: "What you said. Do you actually mean that?"

PARENT: "I can understand why you'd question me. It's a really different thing for me to say – especially when you're not happy about something. You might worry that I'm just making fun or trying to stop you from feeling your feelings."

CHILD: "So do you actually mean it?"

PARENT: "I do mean it. The truth is, I've been thinking about how I react when there is stress or upset feelings in the family. I realized that I'm not always so caring in that way, especially when things are busy. It's something I really want to change. It will feel awkward at first but I'm going to keep practicing because you – my little pixie – are very important to me, and so are your feelings." (reaches out for a tickle)

CHILD: "Ha – stop it"

PARENT: "So – what do you think? Think you can handle it? Any special requests?"

CHILD: "Just don't do it in front of my friends! And make sure you mean what you say!"

PARENT: "Now that is something I can happily do!"

Common Pitfalls

1. "This sounds like a fairytale. I just don't think it's realistic." When we started to write this book, we really wanted it to be less "pie-in-the-sky psycho-babble" and more "true-to-life." It didn't take long to realize though that every family has its unique way of being together. For example, some families are more comfortable with verbal expressions of love than others who may show affection in more physical ways or with humor. Families even have vocabularies that are unique to them. This means that it is vital for you to adapt the structure in a way that fits your personality and your family's culture. We'd still recommend you follow the framework (I can imagine you might feel _____ because × 3 + emotional and practical support) but to do so in a way that feels authentic. That being said, if part of the discomfort lies within the approach – for example, validation is not something you typically offer in certain situations – then we'd urge you to see how you can integrate this skill in a way that feels more comfortable.

2. "I don't think my kid will buy it." Because this is likely to be a very new style of relating to your children, it is possible they may experience it as odd or unnatural, especially if they are older (the younger ones usually eat it up). Sometimes that's just because this new way of communicating is so different, sometimes it's because there's something a little too rehearsed or stilted about the delivery, and sometimes it really is that some older children don't like you trying to understand them so carefully (as you probably already know, it can feel really vulnerable for others to enter into our emotional world). You aren't trying to be a therapist for your kid; you want to have a normal conversation. Unfortunately, for it to become natural, you need time and practice. Sometimes being upfront about that reality can help your loved tolerate the discomfort during the in-between phase.

3. "What if I respond in this way, and they still don't settle?" First things first: Try to compare notes with how it went with the framework as described. If you're confident that your technique was in the "good-enough" domain, then it's possible that a little time and some distance from the issue can help. As much as we believe in the approach, we would be remiss to suggest that it works 100% of the time. It does promote flexibility and connection, though, and so you can count on the fact that your efforts are still helping in some way (that you may not see until later), and at least they aren't hurting. If, when you compare notes, you see that perhaps you were a little off the mark or you missed a step, not a problem – give yourself a bit of a break and circle back for a "do-over."

Reflections

What might make it hard for me to put into words my child's experience in a situation like this?

_____

_____

_____

What might make it hard for me to get practical in a situation like this?

_____

_____

_____

What do I need to deal with a situation like this more confidently in the future?

_____

_____

_____

Part III
Where to from Here?

Parenting is a practice. We learn it though experience – both what we experienced as kids and our own experience as caregivers. What happens once you put down this book? How might you transform what you learned into action? This last section is meant to help you integrate the ideas from the preceding pages into your everyday life. You'll find a summary followed by lots of extra ideas and resources for where to go from here, from suggestions for extra support to opportunities to practice your new skills. Just like children, we parents and caregivers also benefit from having trusted others help us as we navigate the twists and turns and sometimes total chaos of family life. As you read through these next chapters, consider who you already talk to about some of these challenges and whether you'd like to add anyone to your own circle of support.

New Directions 22

We really hope that you've found parts of the book to be applicable to your family life. We set out to capture common parenting moments, since it's usually helpful just to know that these issues arise in households around the world multiple times a day. Parents and caregivers don't often share their kids' worst moments with each other. No one posts a family picture of their kids screaming or fighting each other on social media. Some parents can have honest conversations with their very closest friends and family. Others can only really share the hard stuff anonymously online or in the security of a confidential office with a medical or mental health professional. Many battle through their own daily trenches largely alone. It's only because we have the luxury of talking privately to families every day that we see how universal these struggles are. We can reassure you that no family is as perfect as it seems, no children are as well behaved, and no parents, stepparents, grandparents, etc. have it all figured out. We also have the privilege of seeing the unbelievable dedication and love that parents and caregivers have for their children. Reading this book is just one of the millions of ways, small and large, that you are caring for the young people in your life.

Neither of us ever expected to write a parenting book. We both went into mental health fields wanting to help children. What we discovered professionally is that one of the best ways to help children is to help families get out of stuck patterns of relating to one another – sometimes dating back generations. When we started raising our own children and stepchildren, it became even more obvious how much everyone in the family suffered when our kids were struggling. We also learned that, most often, our kids couldn't change without us taking the lead, and that sometimes meant first getting on the same page with partners in caregiving. It didn't matter how much schooling we had, how many friendships we had with other mental health professionals, or even how much time we'd spent helping other people's kids – nothing could have prepared us for being with the kids in our own lives! Nothing can bring you the same level of joy or frustration or fear or awe. It can be so amazing that we want to hold on forever or so overwhelming that we want to turn away (even run away). When we broke it down into smaller parts, we realized that there were some universal thoughts and worries that get in the way for parents and caregivers, and also some concrete steps to being with a child through all of his or her feelings and behaviors. Inspired by our mentors, colleagues, and the great minds who came before us, we developed the framework outlined in this book to put into words some of those central ideas. We can attest that these practices have definitely made our lives at home easier, and that's why we were so motivated to share them with you.

It's always touching for us to hear parents' stories after they've taken the risk and tried out some of these ideas at home. They often come back and report how their child finally opened up or softened and actually accepted their support. Sometimes, the benefit isn't as obvious, but parents are still trusting in the approach and using the skills. I can think of a mother who recently told me:

> It didn't work. She didn't calm down at all. But I just told her that was okay and that I didn't expect her to be cheerful after such a horrible day. The next day she stayed in the kitchen with me instead of going up to her room and shutting the door like usual. So maybe I did something right?

It's also normal for it to take a few weeks of relating in this new way to notice a difference. Change doesn't tend to happen in a straight line; you may even feel temporary blips or setbacks before things improve, but when parents persist, there is almost always a positive change. You just can't change one part of a relationship pattern without other parts responding in turn. Every action has a reaction, and we count on it!

Let's review a few of the main takeaways. First, it's important, especially at first, to emphasize the use of the three because-statements to pivot from the culturally conditioned responses to try to make our kids' feelings go away. They let your children know that you get them and you're paying attention to their lives. They deepen the validation. They also keep you focused on staying in your children's reality rather than prematurely trying to lead them out of their feeling state.

Figure 22.1 Climbing the mountain of change

It's also important that, as much as possible, the because-statements reflect your child's goodness or positive intention. Even when the behavior isn't so good (e.g., hitting a sibling to get a turn on a video game), you can still reflect the underlying feelings, wishes, or needs (e.g., you were so angry because you felt left out or because you really wanted to have a turn after waiting so long). Reflecting your child in a positive and healthy light lets them see themselves that way. You are their greatest mirror.

The order we've outlined of validation before reassurance or problem-solving (whenever safe to do so) also seems to matter a lot to kids of all ages. In fact, older kids tell us they are much more willing to listen to their parents' advice when they feel understood or accepted first. You can think of it as "Feelings Before Fixing" or "Support Before Solutions." There's the well-known Sylvia Boorstein quote (and book title): "Don't just do something, sit there." She meant to sit first and be with one's own experience before acting, and we essentially mean the same thing for parents with their children. Sitting and listening to them first then providing validation before offering advice is doing something invisible, yet meaningful and powerful.

We recommend following the structure provided until you get your feet under you and then making it your own. Once the principles feel solid (regulate yourself first, see the goodness, feelings before fixing), and you've wrapped your mind around the framework (build a bridge, putting it into words, getting practical), you will automatically convey what you mean to and the details won't matter so much. In other words, don't worry about getting it just right, especially in the beginning when you are acquiring the new skills. It can also be off-putting to kids to see their parent trying to speak to them "perfectly." The focus is best placed on tuning in to yourself and your child, not on the "perfect words to say." If your child feels you are genuine in your efforts, that vulnerable expression of love is the greatest gift you can give your kids, even if you stumble on your words or forget what comes next. And remember, no matter how bad things get – they want you and only you as their mom or dad or stepparent or grandparent. When there is conflict, the intensity of the discord reflects the intensity with which they want you to join them, and help them to get through their toughest moments.

Just like any other new practice, it helps to start with something relatively easy. For example, if you routinely love celebrating your child's joy with her, you can just tack on some of the "putting it into words" stuff. If you're more comfortable with your child's anxiety, start with applying your new tools in these situations before moving into the more angry zones. If you have more than one child, it can also work well to start with the child whom you think will respond better. It's not always going to go well, but every time you do it, you are making a long-term investment in your relationship with your child and their brain development. Not only will this way of responding help your children in the moment, but, over time, they will internalize the framework, and this will help them tremendously in their life as they use it themselves and with the other people around them. In other words, when you change your way of being with your child, you change the DNA of the relationship, and that gets passed along the generations. Sometimes – when I am tired and frustrated and the last thing I want to do is build a bridge (never mind put it into words) – I think of the generations past who did their best to parent us with the little science and support they had access to at the time. Then I get back up again in their honor to untangle some of those intergenerational cycles. Now if that doesn't resonate with you, totally okay, find the meaning in your efforts so that you can draw from that well when you are struggling with the day-to-day. Sometimes consciously bringing to mind the big picture can give us perspective and take the edge off in the moment.

If you're a bit hesitant about how this will all go, please don't forget the "do-over." At the start, 95% of your efforts may be "do-overs." The first step is realizing that the interaction didn't go as hoped *after* the interaction. We're serious – that's awesome. "Do-overs" can honestly be just as good as staying calm or present the first time. It would be weird to always be fully tuned into your child's feelings or needs. It's neither possible nor good for children if you "get it" all the time. Those gaps when parents are out of sync with their child help build a child's autonomy and resilience to stress, and reconnection teaches the child that the parent–child bond is strong enough to withstand everyday wear and tear. In other words, healthy relationships are all about missing the mark and then course correction. This can mean a "do-over" with a specific interaction or even a commitment to a new way of relating altogether. These are helpful in all relationships, whether at home or elsewhere. They are especially useful in co-parenting where emotions tend to run pretty high when the going gets tough or when the family structure is changing. You can use these principles to work more effectively as a team with your partners in caregiving, and it will lower not only your stress but your child's as well. In fact, sometimes co-parenting disagreements or stress are one of the main factors that get in the way of parents being able to build a bridge to Child Island. Your mind can only be in so many places at once! It is much easier to parent when you feel supported (or at least not distracted by) your co-parent. If you don't feel your co-parent's support, we urge you to "be the first domino." It doesn't always feel good or "fair," especially if you feel like you're always the one to have to take the lead, but every action really does have a reaction and your efforts will prove fruitful over time, especially if you are sincere in your intentions. Trust us on this one – we have had the opportunity to work with many partners in caregiving who were struggling to be in the same room, never mind "get on the same page" with respect to their kids and what we've learned is that the pain fueling both sides is most often rooted in vulnerability – fear, hurt, even shame. When this vulnerable pain can be met with kindness and support, and with no expectation for anything in return (even if just for the kids' sake at first), magic can happen.

As parents start to focus in on listening to their children differently, they often become aware of all the inner and external distractions: work stress, overscheduling, electronics buzzing. The pace of life and the overall stress load starts to feel at odds with the deep desire to connect with our children in a helpful and meaningful way. Many parents start by focusing on communication with their children and develop more interest in knowing more about stress reduction for themselves. If you're in this boat, you are not alone. Our generation of parents have so much on our minds. There are constant demands on our resources and attention. There are also new challenges (like our children's digital immersion) and anxieties (like our kids' economic and environmental future). Fortunately, we are also at a time when mindfulness practice has become mainstream, and there are many options for busy parents. All of the ancient traditions teach a form of mindfulness or "paying attention, on purpose, nonjudgmentally." Nowadays, it is possible to find guidance around mindfulness practice from many sources: podcasts, books, secular teachers, religious teachers, and retreats. When I (Ashley) was first having a hard time as a new parent, my mentor and colleague suggested mindfulness practice. Of all the things I've learned and tried, mindfulness meditation has been the simplest, cheapest, and most helpful approach to managing my own stress as a parent. Our favorite title for a mindfulness book is Dan Harris's *Meditation for Fidgety Skeptics* because, in real life, who likes the idea of sitting still and having to focus on your own breathing with so much going on in the background? Not too many parents, especially parents who are already tearing their hair out. If you can relate, we want you to know that there are many ways to practice mindfulness in daily life that don't involve sitting still for 30 minutes at a time (for real!). For more information, check out the resources section for some recommended books and websites. One we particularly love is *Mindful Parent, Mindful Child: Simple Mindfulness Practices for Busy Parents*, an audiobook by Susan Kaiser Greenland.

If you're interested in a group format program (a good excuse to get out of the house once a week), there are several options.

The first secular mindfulness program was pioneered by Jon Kabat-Zinn and is called **Mindfulness-based stress reduction**. This course is available in many urban centers and some online formats. It's a great introduction to mindfulness practice and helps participants become more aware of and less reactive to everyday events.

Mindfulness-based parent training is an offshoot of Mindfulness-Based Stress Reduction designed specifically for parents. This can be especially useful if your child is suffering from a medical or mental health condition or you are dealing with stress that is particularly related to parenting.

Mindful self-compassion deepens practices that are usually introduced in other mindfulness training. As we discussed in Chapter 4, self-compassion practices can help us deal with parenting challenges, as we aren't easily able to take space away from the issue. It is the antidote to all the unrealistic expectations faced by many parents today. We highly recommend it.

Mindfulness-based cognitive therapy is geared toward people with anxiety or depression. It has been shown to be helpful for new parents and for anyone with recurrent bouts of depression.

Maybe you're looking for something more in terms of parenting support or your child is struggling with a behavioral issue or mental health issue and you could benefit from "advanced caregiving skills." If so, we agree with other authors like Brené Brown who suggest that parents don't need "experts" to give advice so much as they need space to uncover and listen to their own inner wisdom. I (Adele) am definitely biased in thinking that **emotion-focused family therapy (EFFT)** can be helpful, as I am a co-developer of the approach. The framework captured in this book shares common roots, and the focus of EFFT is to support parents with skills and strategies to help their kids with behaviors, emotions, and their relationship. Should parents' efforts to support their child get blocked by their fear (of making things worse), self-blame (for their child's struggles), or other thoughts or feelings (hopelessness, grief, etc.), the EFFT therapist helps the parent to reconnect to their caregiving instincts and get back on track. Check out www.emotion-focusedfamilytherapy.org for links to a number of free videos for parents and caregivers inspired by the approach.

Traditional **family therapy** (where two or more members of the family typically come together) is another way to get "in-person" support to have more understanding and less conflict in the family and to put into practice some of the ideas and tools described in this book. Many parents worry that a referral for "family therapy" means "it must be the parents' fault." We believe just the opposite: Parents can be the biggest part of the solution, even if things have been really hard for a long while. Family therapy helps parents and kids get out of stuck patterns of relating and connect with each other in ways that better meet each family member's needs.

Many communities offer **parent guidance and support**, either through in-person groups or telephone/video-coaching. You can always ask your primary care provider, health unit and/or local school for recommendations. These resources are often convenient, affordable and based on sound research evidence.

Finally, parenthood can really shake things up emotionally, so it's not surprising that parents often become interested in understanding more about themselves or their other relationships. There is a wide range of support out there for parents, from online peer support groups to counseling and psychotherapy. For example, **individual psychotherapy** can be really helpful to become more aware of your thoughts and feelings and improve relationships with your kids, your co-parent, and other important others. Contrary to popular belief, psychotherapy doesn't have to be a deep exploration of your own childhood unless you want it to be. Those interested in how childhood experiences may influence their current efforts as a parent or who are now trying to give their children experiences that they never received but wished they had, **psychodynamic psychotherapy** may be an ideal choice. **Cognitive behavioral therapy** is also widely available, is usually short-term, and focuses on "here-and-now" issues, such as negative thinking patterns and how to change them in day-to-day life. **Interpersonal psychotherapy** helps parents identify their feelings in the context of important relationships and improve communication with significant others. **Couples therapy** can be especially useful for co-parents and may center on supporting each other in your parenting role. Working on the couple relationship is often helpful to children but doesn't need to be the main focus if you don't want it to be. There are many other forms of psychotherapy, and in the end, the relationship with the therapist is probably the most important factor in getting the support you want.

One additional form of support I may pursue is:

A Final Word

When it feels like you've tried everything and nothing seems to work, it's easy to lose hope. It can make you worry that something is really wrong with your child, yourself or your relationship. Hopefully, as you've used some of the ideas in this book, you've seen more glimmers of connection and calm. If not, then rest assured that change can take time. Children are incredibly resilient creatures. So are parents and caregivers. We are programmed to learn and grow together. No matter what your child has been through or how she is reacting right now, there is always, always hope. The bond between a child and their primary caregiver is stronger than it seems, and children want things to get better. Your child likely won't yet be able to thank you for all that you are doing or to tell you that even when things go sideways, he appreciates how you stick by him again and again. We hope that in the meantime, you can give yourself credit for being willing to try out new things, fall, and get back up again. It is a tremendous gift you are giving yourself and your child and we so firmly believe that your efforts are incredibly meaningful.

Practical Resources   **23**

In case you'd like a little more practice to figure out what will work best for you and your child, we've included a template to build your own road map. It can be applied to any situation that might arise. In this chapter, you'll find a brief summary and then a few pages of examples for different situations. At the end of the chapter, you can also find tables with more information relating to feelings with more information on how to adapt this content to your child or family's unique needs.

1. Your Quick Guide for What to Say to Kids …

Once you've built a bridge to Child Island and you have at least a couple of ideas to make sense of your child's experience, you can use the following guide to figure out how you might want to approach any given situation:

 Putting It into Words

A. Convey understanding of their experience:

I could understand that you …
I could imagine that you …
No wonder you …
It would make sense that you …

When I put myself in your shoes, I could see why you …
… might feel/think/want to/not want to _____

B. Demonstrate that you "get it":
because 1: _____ because 2: _____ because 3: _____

 **Getting Practical**

Emotional Support Ideas

- Offer comfort in words or with physical affection ("Come here and I'll give you a hug")
- Provide reassurance ("I believe it will be okay")
- Communicate acceptance and non-judgment ("It's totally normal to feel that way")
- Communicate togetherness and availability ("We're in this together," "I'm here for you")
- Communicate trust or belief in the child, his abilities, his good intentions ("I believe you can get through this")
- Share enjoyment with your child ("Wow – that is so cool!")
- Allow space (space can be physical or psychological *and* time-limited; the plan for reconnection must be clearly communicated ("Why don't I give you some space and I'll check back in with you in 5 minutes")

Practical Support Ideas

- Redirect your child to another thought or activity (e.g., playing a game, engaging in a physical activity, listening to music)
- Teach and practice communication and social skills (e.g. teaching assertiveness)
- Teach and practice mindfulness, self-compassion and relaxation skills (e.g. noticing the red objects in the room; reminding the child that everyone struggles sometimes; belly breathing)
- Support your child to face fears (e.g. doing difficult things with exposures to the anxiety-provoking thing or situation in a gradual, step-by-step way)
- Use positive reinforcement (e.g. praising and/or rewarding desirable behaviors)
- Help your child to brainstorm ideas for a solution (e.g. taking turns coming up with possible ideas)
- Offer solutions to help solve the practical problem or take over to solve the problem (e.g. suggesting that this is a problem that needs adult help)
- Offer a few choices or some degree of control over the situation (e.g. narrowing the options for the child)
- Set a limit (e.g. being clear about expectations or what needs to happen)
- Just be with your child and let the feelings run their course

2. Guideposts

Some of the examples in this section will be familiar from the book and others are meant to represent common parenting situations that we didn't include. They are organized by the child's communication into a few sections: refusals, wishes, feeling states and relationship-based comments.

I Don't Want to…

I don't want to get out of bed.
Building a Bridge (reasons why your child might not want to get out of bed):

1.

2.

3.

Putting It into Words (using language that suits your child's age and personality):
I can understand why you might not want to get out of bed because:

1.

2.

3.

Getting Practical
Emotional support sentences:

Practical support suggestions:

I don't want to go to school.
Building a Bridge (reasons why your child might not want to go to school):

1.

2.

3.

Putting It into Words (using language that suits your child's age and personality):
I could imagine you might not want to go to school because:

1.

2.

3.

Getting Practical
Emotional support sentences:

Practical support suggestions:

I don't want to come for dinner.
Building a Bridge (reasons why your child might not want to come for dinner):

1.

2.

3.

Putting It into Words (using language that suits your child's age and personality):
No wonder you might not want to come for dinner because:

1.

2.

3.

Getting Practical
Emotional support sentences:

Practical support suggestions:

I don't want to do my homework.
Building a Bridge (reasons why your child might not want to do homework):

1.

2.

3.

Putting It into Words (using language that suits your child's age and personality):
It would make sense to me why you might not want to go to do your homework because:

1.

2.

3.

Getting Practical
Emotional support sentences:

Practical support suggestions:

I don't want you to have another baby.
Building a Bridge (reasons why your child might not want you to have another baby):

1.

2.

3.

Putting It into Words (using language that suits your child's age and personality):
Of course you might not want us to have another baby because:

1.

2.

3.

Getting Practical
Emotional support sentences:

Practical support suggestions:

I don't want …
Building a Bridge (reasons why your child might not want _____):

1.

2.

3.

Putting It into Words (using language that suits your child's age and personality):
When I put myself in your shoes, I can see why you might not want _____ because:

1.

2.

3.

Getting Practical
Emotional support sentences:

Practical support suggestions:

I Want To …

I want to stay up later.
Building a Bridge (reasons why your child might want to stay up later):

1.

2.

3.

Putting It into Words (using language that suits your child's age and personality):
I can understand why you would want to stay up later because:

1.

2.

3.

Getting Practical
Emotional support sentences:

Practical support suggestions:

I want that toy.
Building a Bridge (reasons why your child might want that toy):

1.

2.

3.

Putting It into Words (using language that suits your child's age and personality):
I can imagine why you would want that toy because:

1.

2.

3.

Getting Practical
Emotional support sentences:

Practical support suggestions:

I want to run away.
Building a Bridge (reasons why your child might want to run away):

1.

2.

3.

Putting It into Words (using language that suits your child's age and personality):
No wonder you would want to run away because:

1.

2.

3.

Getting Practical
Emotional support sentences:

Practical support suggestions:

I Want …

Building a Bridge (reasons why your child might want _____):

1.

2.

3.

Putting It into Words (using language that suits your child's age and personality):
I can understand why you would want _____ because:

1.

2.

3.

Getting Practical
Emotional support sentences:

Practical support suggestions:

I feel ...
Mad

Building a Bridge (reasons why your child might feel mad):

1.

2.

3.

Putting It into Words (using language that suits your child's age and personality):
When I put myself in your shoes, I can see why you might feel mad because:

1.

2.

3.

Getting Practical
Emotional support sentences:

Practical support suggestions:

Sad

Building a Bridge (reasons why your child might feel sad):

1.

2.

3.

Putting It into Words (using language that suits your child's age and personality):
I can understand why you might feel sad because:

1.

2.

3.

Getting Practical
Emotional support sentences:

Practical support suggestions:

Scared

Building a Bridge (reasons why your child might feel scared):

1.

2.

3.

Putting It into Words (using language that suits your child's age and personality):
I can imagine why you might feel scared because:

1.

2.

3.

Getting Practical
Emotional support sentences:

Practical support suggestions:

Embarrassed

Building a Bridge (reasons why your child might feel embarrassed):

1.

2.

3.

Putting It into Words (using language that suits your child's age and personality):
Of course you might feel embarrassed because:

1.

2.

3.

Getting Practical
Emotional support sentences:

Practical support suggestions:

Happy

Building a Bridge (reasons why your child might feel happy):

1.

2.

3.

Putting It into Words (using language that suits your child's age and personality):
No wonder you might feel happy because:

1.

2.

3.

Getting Practical
Emotional support sentences:

Practical support suggestions:

... (Other Feeling Word)

Building a Bridge (reasons why your child might feel _____):

1.

2.

3.

Putting It into Words (using language that suits your child's age and personality):
I get why you might feel _____ because:

1.

2.

3.

Getting Practical
Emotional support sentences:

Practical support suggestions:

Relationship with Parent/Caregiver
I hate you.

Building a Bridge (reasons why your child might be angry with you):

1.

2.

3.

Putting It into Words (using language that suits your child's age and personality):
It makes sense to me that you might be angry with me because:

1.

2.

3.

Getting Practical
Emotional support sentences:

Practical support suggestions:

Why are you talking to me like that?

Building a Bridge (reasons why your child might respond with discomfort or mistrust to your efforts to validate their perspective):

1.

2.

3.

Putting It into Words (using language that suits your child's age and personality):
I can understand why you would say that because:

1.

2.

3.

Getting Practical
Emotional support sentences:

Practical support suggestions:

Silence

Building a Bridge (reasons why your child might not want to talk to you about this topic):

1.

2.

3.

Putting It into Words (using language that suits your child's age and personality):
When I put myself in your shoes, I can see why you wouldn't want to talk to me about this because:

1.

2.

3.

Getting Practical
Emotional support sentences:

Practical support suggestions:

...

Building a Bridge (reasons why your child might …):

1.

2.

3.

Putting It into Words (using language that suits your child's age and personality):
I could imagine why you … because:

1.

2.

3.

Getting Practical
Emotional support sentences:

Practical support suggestions:

3. Feelings Quick Sheet

Here are some examples of the types of physical sensations and actions that come along with different core emotions. Research has shown that these physical elements are similar across genders and cultures, even though the ways we show them on the outside may vary from person to person. Kids may not notice emotions as easily as adults or think of them as clearly separate from each other. They learn that as they grow and with adult support.

Feelings In the Body

	Joy	Sadness	Fear	Shame	Anger
Body sensation	Floating, light or expanding	Lump in throat, hollow, heavy or empty feeling	Shaking, tight muscles, sore stomach, tingly feelings, hot/cold, fast heart rate	Sinking feeling, queasiness feeling flushed, hunching	Tight muscles, clenched fists, fast heart rate
Body Location	Whole body, chest, head	Throat, chest, belly, legs and arms	Belly, head, face, chest, throat	Chest, head, eyes	Head, shoulders, arms, hands
Action/ Impulse	Want to celebrate, share joy with someone, smile	Want to cry, curl up in a ball, get a hug, lie down	Want to escape, run and hide, freeze or fight	Want to hide, cover face, escape	Want to hit or yell, break or throw something, take space

It can be helpful to run through this table adding or deleting sensations that apply to you, so you can become even more aware of how emotions show up in your own body. This will also help you teach your child to do the same.

An extra tip: If your child doesn't yet identify with a certain emotion or might be overwhelmed or embarrassed by you naming it – for example, with anger – it's okay to tone down the intensity of the word you use to describe it. Instead of saying, "I can understand why you'd be angry …," you can say, "I can imagine why you'd be upset/annoyed/frustrated."

You can also take the word and separate it from the child; for example: "Anyone would be angry/upset/annoyed/frustrated in this situation." You can also avoid the feeling word altogether at first and comment on the body sensation or action: "If I put myself in your shoes, I'd want to throw that paper in the garbage!" or "I can imagine it would make your fists curl/blood boil/head explode to think that …" You can express also your understand of their thoughts, beliefs, or what they say rather than feelings. For example: "No wonder you think Annie is annoying, because …" or "I can imagine why you'd say Jess doesn't like you because …"

Ideally, you can aim to increase your use of "feelings words" because these will give children more specific language to describe their own experience. As we mentioned earlier in the book, when children can identify the body sensations linked to their emotions and use feelings words (in their own minds or to communicate them to others) enough of the time, it's likely that the outbursts, behavior problems, and meltdowns will fade away. This is a lifelong learning process for most of us.

Sample Feelings Words

	Joy	Sadness	Fear Anxiety	Shame	Anger
Strong	Overjoyed Excited Thrilled Delighted	Despairing Hopeless Empty Helpless	Horrified Petrified Panicked Paralyzed	Humiliated Mortified Disgraced Degraded	Furious Outraged Irate Fuming
Moderate	Happy Up In high spirits	Awful Blue Miserable Upset Lonely Sad	Freaked-out Scared Worried Nervous Afraid	Embarrassed Lost face Disrespected Taken down	Angry Resentful Ticked off Mad
Light	Glad Satisfied Content	Low Blah Disappointed Unhappy	On edge Cautious Tense Uncertain	Flustered Shy Uncomfortable	Annoyed Irritated Bothered

Recommended Readings

24

This chapter lists a number of resources for different issues faced by families with kids of varying ages. They are organized according to different categories and we made efforts to include resources that we believe are useful and that families have appreciated. We hope they will provide you with a starting point for a variety of challenges common to families today. That being said, this list is not meant to be comprehensive, and over time, new and more up-to-date resources will be published that reflect advances in clinical science and practice.

Anxiety and School Refusal

Parents

Chansky, T.E., 2004. *Freeing your child from anxiety: Powerful, practical strategies to overcome your child's fears, phobias, and worries*. Harmony Books.

Eisen, A.R. and Engler, L.B., 2006. *Helping your child overcome separation anxiety or school refusal: A step-by-step guide for parents*. New Harbinger Publications.

Haarman, G.B., 2011. *School refusal behaviour: Children who can't or won't go to school*. Education and Consultation Press, Louisville.

Lebowitz, E.R. and Omer, H., 2013. *Treating childhood and adolescent anxiety: A guide for caregivers*. John Wiley & Sons.

Manassis, K., 2008. *Keys to parenting your anxious child*. Barron's Educational Series.

Rapee, R., Wignall, A., Spence, S., Lyneham, H., and Cobham, V. 2008. *Helping your anxious child: A step-by-step guide for parents*. New Harbinger Publications.

Spencer, E.D., DuPont, R.L., and DuPont, C.M. 2003. *The anxiety cure for kids: A guide for parents*. John Wiley & Sons.

Wagner, A.P., 2002. *Worried no more: Help and hope for anxious children*. Lighthouse Press.

Children

Bains, G.A., Bains, P., and Gianoglio, J. 2009. *A child's story: Going to school with anxiety*. AuthorHouse.

Crist, J.J., 2004. *What to do when you're scared & worried: A guide for kids*. Free Spirit Publishing.

Garland, E.J. and Clark, S.L. 2000. *Taming worry dragons: A manual for children, parents, and other coaches*. Mood and Anxiety Disorders Clinic, Department of Psychiatry, British Columbia's Children's Hospital.

Huebner, D. and Matthews, B. 2006. *What to do when you worry too much: A kid's guide to overcoming anxiety*. Magination Press.

Lavallee, K., and Schneider, S. 2017. *What to do when you don't want to be apart: A kid's guide to overcoming separation anxiety*. Magination Press.

Penn, A. 2007. *The kissing hand*. Tanglewood.

Spencer, E.D., DuPont, R.L., and DuPont, C.M. 2014. *The anxiety cure for kids: A guide for parents and children*. John Wiley & Sons.

Attention-Deficit/Hyperactivity Disorder (ADHD) and Learning Differences

Parents

Barkley, R. 2013. *Taking charge of ADHD, Third Edition: The complete, authoritative guide for parents*. Guilford Press.

Dawson, P., and Guare, R. 2009. Smart but scattered: The revolutionary "executive skills" approach to helping kids reach their potential. Guilford Press.

Franklin, D. 2018. *Helping your child with language-based learning disabilities: Strategies to succeed in school & life with dyslexia, dysgraphia, dyscalculia, ADHD & processing disorders*. New Harbinger.

Children

Esham, B., Gordon, M., and Gordon, C. 2015. *Mrs. Gorski, I think I have the wiggle fidgets*. Little Pickle Press.

Miles, B.S., Patterson, C., and Heinrichs, J. 2014. *How I learn: A kid's guide to learning disability*. Magination Press.

Taylor, J. 2013. *The survival guide for kids with ADHD* (updated edition). Free Spirit Publishing.

Assertive Anger

Parents

Golden, B. 2006. *Healthy anger: How to help children and teens manage their anger*. Oxford University Press.

Children

Schab, L. 2009. *Cool, calm, and confident: A workbook to help kids learn assertiveness skills*. Instant Help.
Whitson, S. 2011. *How to be angry: An assertive anger expression group guide for kids and teens*. Jessica Kingsley Publishers.

Blending Families

Parents

Deal, R.L., and Olson, D.H. 2015. *The smart stepfamily marriage: Keys to success in the blended family*. Baker Books.
LeBey, B. 2005. *Remarried with children: Ten secrets for successfully blending and extending your family*. Bantam.
Mullineaux, T.C., and Karinch, M., 2016. *Blending families: Merging households with kids 8–18*. Rowman & Littlefield.
Shimberg, E.F. 1999. Blending families: A guide for parents, stepparents, grandparents and everyone building a successful new family. Penguin.

Children

Harris, R.H. 2012. *Who's in my family: All about our families*. Candlewick.
Ricci, I. 2006. *Mom's house, Dad's house for kids: Feeling at home in one home or two*. Touchstone.
Winnett, E. 2014. Mom or Dad's house?: A workbook to help kids cope with divorce. Counseling with HEART.

Bullying

Parents

Anthony, M., and Lindert, R. 2010. *Little girls can be mean: Four steps to bully-proof girls in the early grades*. St. Martin's Griffin.

Borba, M. 2016. *UnSelfie: Why empathetic kids succeed in our all-about-me world.* Simon and Schuster.

Dellasega, C., and Nixon, C., 2007. *Girl wars: 12 strategies that will end female bullying.* Simon and Schuster.

Goldman, C., and Postel, D. 2012. *Bullied: What every parent, teacher, and kid needs to know about ending the cycle of fear.* HarperOne.

Gordon, M. 2009. *Roots of empathy: Changing the world child by child.* The Experiment.

Hurley, K. 2018. *No more mean girls: The secret to raising strong, confident, and compassionate girls.* Penguin.

Rigby, K. 2008. *Children and bullying: How parents and educators can reduce bullying at school.* Blackwell Publishing.

Simmons, R., 2002. *Odd girl out: The hidden culture of aggression in girls.* Houghton Mifflin Harcourt.

Children

Criswell, P.K. 2009. *Stand up for yourself & your friends: Dealing with bullies & bossiness and finding a better way.* American Girl.

Lohmann, R.C., and Taylor, J.V. 2013. *The bullying workbook for teens: Activities to help you deal with social aggression and cyberbullying.* New Harbinger.

Simmons, R., 2004. *Odd girl speaks out: Girls write about bullies, cliques, popularity, and jealousy.* Houghton Mifflin Harcourt.

Whitson, S. 2011. *Friendship and other weapons: Group activities to help young girls aged 5–11 to cope with bullying.* Jessica Kingsley Publishers.

Challenging Behavior

Parents

Greene, R.W., 2014. *The explosive child: A new approach for understanding and parenting easily frustrated, chronically inflexible children.* HarperCollins.

Greene, R.W., 2009. *Lost at school: Why our kids with behavioral challenges are falling through the cracks and how we can help them.* Simon and Schuster.

Children

Cook, J. 2015. *But it's not my fault.* Boys Town Press.

Smith, B. 2016. *What were you thinking?: Learning to control your impulses.* Boys Town Press.

Co-parent/Couple Relationships

Gottman, J and DeClaire, J. 2002. *The relationship cure: A 5 step guide to strengthening your marriage, family, and friendships.* Three Rivers Press.

Johnson, Sue. 2008. *Hold me tight: Seven conversations for a lifetime of love*. Little, Brown Spark.

Lerner, H. 2017. *Why won't you apologize?: Healing big betrayals and everyday hurts*. Gallery Books.

Depression and Suicide

Parents

Barnard, M.U. 2003. *Helping your depressed child: A step-by-step guide for parents*. New Harbinger.

Cartwright-Hatton, S., 2007. *Coping with an anxious or depressed child*. Oneworld Publications.

Eyers, K. and Parker, G., 2010. *Navigating teenage depression: A guide for parents and professionals*. Routledge.

Fitzpatrick, C. and Sharry, J., 2004 *Coping with depression in young people: A guide for parents*. John Wiley & Sons.

Riley, D.A., 2001. *Depressed child: A parent's guide for rescuing kids*. Taylor Trade Publishing.

Serani, D., 2013. *Depression and your child: A guide for parents and caregivers*. Rowman & Littlefield.

American Academy of Child and Adolescent Psychiatry, 2019. *Suicide resource center*. [online] Available at: www.aacap.org/aacap/families_and_youth/resource_centers/Suicide_Resource_Center/Home.aspx#getting_help

Centre for Suicide Prevention. 2019. *Youth at risk: How to talk to a suicidal teen*. Centre for Suicide Prevention [online] Available at: www.suicideinfo.ca/youth-risk-adults [Accessed 20 April 2019].

American Academy of Child and Adolescent Psychiatry "Threats by children: When are they serious?" [online] Available at: <www.aacap.org/AACAP/Families_and_Youth/Facts_for_Families/FFF-Guide/Childrens-Threats-When-Are-They-Serious-065.aspx≥ [Accessed 19 April 2019].

Kelty Mental Health Resource Centre, 2019. *Suicide*. BC Children's Hospital. [online]. Available at: <https://keltymentalhealth.ca/node/4096≥ [Accessed 20 April 2019].

Children

Cook, J., 2012. *Blueloon*. National Center for Youth Issues.

Foley, J., 2016. *Danny and the blue cloud: Coping with childhood depression*. Magination Press.

Fusek, A. and Peters, P., 2014. *The colour thief*. Hachette Children's Group.

Greive, B.T., 2005. *The blue day book for kids*. Andres McMeel Publishing.

Hamail, S.W., 2004. *My feeling better workbook: Activities that help kids beat the blues*. Instant Help Publications.

Toner, J., 2016. *Depression: A teen's guide to survive and thrive*. Magination.
Weissman, J., 2009. *Can I catch it like a cold? Coping with a parent's depression*. Tundra
   Books.

Eating Disorders

Parents

Boachie, A. and Jasper, K., 2011. *A parent's guide to defeating eating disorders: Spotting
   the stealth bomber and other symbolic approaches*. Jessica Kingsley Publishers.
Bryant-Waugh, R., 2019. *ARFID Avoidant Restrictive Food Intake Disorder: A guide for
   parents and carers*. Routledge.
Lock, J. and Le Grange, D., 2015. *Help your teenager beat an eating disorder*. Guilford
   Publications.

Gender and LGBTQ+ Issues

Parents

Dohrenwend, A., 2012. *Coming around: Parenting lesbian, gay, bisexual, and transgen-
   der kids*. New Horizon Press.

Children

Gino, A. 2015. *George*. Scholastic Press.
Thorn, T. 2019. *It feels good to be yourself: A book about gender identity*. Henry Holt and Co.

General Parenting and Emotion Regulation

Brown, Brené. 2015. *The gifts of imperfect parenting: Raising children with courage,
   compassion, and connection*. (audiobook). Sounds True.
Chapman, G. and Campbell, R., 2016. *The 5 love languages of children: The secret to
   loving children effectively*. Moody Publishers.
Hoffman, K., Cooper, G., and Powell, B., 2017. *Raising a secure child: How circle of se-
   curity parenting can help you nurture your child's attachment, emotional resilience,
   and freedom to explore*. The Guilford Press.
Gottman, J.M., 2004. *What am I feeling?* Parenting Press, Inc.
Gottman, J., 2011. *Raising an emotionally intelligent child*. Simon and Schuster.
Faber, A. and Mazlish, E. 1980. *How to talk so kids will listen and listen so kids will talk*.
   Scribner.

Harvey, P. and Penzo, J.A., 2009. *Parenting a child who has intense emotions: Dialectical behavior therapy skills to help your child regulate emotional outbursts and aggressive behaviors*. New Harbinger Publications.
Kang, S. 2014. *The dolphin way: A parent's guide to raising healthy, happy, and motivated kids-without turning into a tiger*. Viking Canada.
Neufeld, G. and Maté, G., 2004. *Hold onto your kids: Why parents need to matter more than peers*. New York, NY: Vintage Canada.
Paley, V.G., 2009. *A child's work: The importance of fantasy play*. University of Chicago Press.
Siegel, D.J. and Bryson, T.P., 2012. *The whole-brain child: 12 revolutionary strategies to nurture your child's developing mind*. Bantam.
Siegel, D.J. and Bryson, T.P., 2016. *No drama discipline: The whole-brain way to calm the chaos and nurture your child's developing mind*. Random House.
Siegel, D.J. and Bryson, T.P., 2019. *The yes brain: How to cultivate courage, curiosity, and resilience in your child*. Bantam.
Siegel, D.J. and Hartzell, M., 2004. *Parenting from the inside out: How a deeper self-understanding can help you raise children who thrive*. Jeremy P. Tarcher/Penguin.
https://www.mentalhealthfoundations.ca
https://www.emotionfocusedfamilytherapy.org
https://www.ahaparenting.com/

Grief

Parents

Balk, D. 2010. *Children's encounters with death, bereavement, and coping*. Springer Publishing Company.
Coloroso, B. 2000. *Parenting through crisis: Helping kids in times of loss, grief, and change*. HarperCollins Publishers.
Emswiler, M.A., and James P.E. 2000. *Guiding your child through grief*. Bantam.
Fitzgerald, H. 2013. *The grieving child: A parent's guide*. Simon and Schuster.
Manning, M., and Patterson, J. 1999. *35 Ways To Help A Grieving Child*. Dougy Center.
Schaefer, D. 2011. *How do we tell the children?: A step-by-step guide for helping children two to teen cope when someone dies*. ReadHowYouWant. com.
Silverman, P.R. and Kelly, M. 2009. *A parent's guide to raising grieving children: rebuilding your family after the death of a loved one*. Oxford University Press, USA.

Children

Cook, J. 2011. *Grief is like a snowflake*. National Center for Youth Issues.
Leutenbergm E. and Zamore, F. 2012. *GriefWork for teens: Healing from loss*. Whole Person Associates.
Leeuwenburgh, E. and Goldring, E. 2008. *Why did you die?: Activities to help children cope with grief and loss*. New Harbinger Publications.

McWhorter, G. 2005. *Healing activities for children in grief*. Gary McWorter.
Schmidt, R. 2011. *65 Healing activities and CD*. Marco Products.

Media and Electronics

Parents

Lloyds Lender, W. 2014. *A practical guide to parenting in the digital age: How to nurture safe, balanced, and connected children and teens*. CreateSpace Independent Publishing Platform.
Uhls, Y.T. 2016. *Media moms & digital dads: A fact-not-fear approach to parenting in the digital age*. Routledge.

Mindfulness and Mindful Parenting

Parents

Kaiser Greenland, Susan. 2019. *Mindful parent, mindful child: Simple mindfulness practices for busy parents*. Sounds True.
Stiffelman, S. 2015. *Parenting with presence: Practices for raising conscious, confident, caring kids*. New World Library.
Willard, C. 2017. *Raising Resilience: The wisdom and science of happy families and thriving children*. Sounds True.
Kabat-Zinn, J and Kabat-Zinn, M. 1998. *Everyday blessings: The inner work of mindful parenting*. Hachetter Books.

Children

Garcia, G. 2017. *Listening to my body: A guide to helping kids understand the connection between their sensations (what the heck are those?) and feelings so that they can get better at figuring out what they need*. Skinned Knee Publishing.
Vo, Dzung X. 2015. *The mindful teen: Powerful skills to help you handle stress one moment at a time*. Raincoast Books.

Perfectionism

Parents

Adderholdt, M. and Goldberg, J. 1999. *Perfectionism: What's bad about being too good? Revised and updated edition*. Free Spirit Publishing Inc.

Homayoun, A. 2012. *The myth of the perfect girl: Helping our daughters find authentic success and happiness in school and life*. Penguin.

Jay, M. 2017. *Supernormal: The untold story of adversity and resilience*. Twelve.

Smith, J. 2017. *Untying parent anxiety: 18 myths that have you in knots – and how to get free*. Familius.

Children

Adderholdt, M. and Goldberg, J. 1999. *Perfectionism: What's bad about being too good?* Free Spirit Publishing.

Burns, E., 2008. *Nobody's perfect: A story for children about perfectionism*. Magination Press.

Greenspoon, T. 2007. *What to do when good enough isn't good: The real deal in perfectionism: A guide for kids*. Free Spirit Publishing.

Pett, M., 2011. *The girl who never made mistakes*. Sourcebooks Jabberwocky.

John, J. 2019. *The good egg*. HarperCollins Children's Books.

Physical Symptoms and Mind–Body Connection

Parents

American Academy of Child and Adolescent Psychiatry. 2017. *Physical symptoms of emotional distress: Somatic symptoms and related disorders*. [online] Available at <www.aacap.org/AACAP/Families_and_Youth/Facts_for_Families/FFF-Guide/Physical_Symptoms_of_Emotional_Distress-Somatic_Symptoms_and_Related_Disorders.aspx> [Accessed 20 April 2019].

Children

Green, K. and Penner, C. n.d. Sam's Journey: A Story of Somatization [online] Available at: https://keltymentalhealth.ca/sites/default/files/resources/Sam%27s%20Journey.pdf

Resilience and Self-Compassion

Parents

Brown, B. 2015. *Daring greatly: How the courage to be vulnerable transforms the way we Live, love, parent, and lead*. Penguin Random House.

Carlsson-Paige, N. 2008. *Taking back childhood: A proven roadmap for raising confident, creative, compassionate kids*. Penguin.

Siegel, D.J. and Hartzell, M. 2013. *Parenting from the inside out: How a deeper self-understanding can help you raise children who thrive*. TarcherPerigee.

Young-Eisendrath, P. 2008. *The self-esteem trap: Raising confident and compassionate kids in an age of self-importance*. Little, Brown.

Children

Bradshaw, C.M. 2016. *How to like yourself: A teen's guide to quieting your inner critic and building lasting self-esteem*. New Harbinger Publications.

Gadeberg, J. 1997. *Brave new girls*. Fairview Press.

Garcia, G. 2017. *Listening with my heart: A story of kindness and self-compassion*. Skinned Knee Publishing.

Krouse Rosenthal, A. and Rosenthal, P. 2017. *Dear girl*. HarperCollins.

Moss, W.L. 2010. *Being me: A kid's guide to boosting confidence and self-esteem*. Magination Press.

Taylor, J.V. 2014. *The body image workbook for teens: Activities to help girls develop a healthy body image in an image-obsessed world*. New Harbinger Publications.

Tyler, M., 2005. *The skin you live in*. Chicago Children's Museum.

Zobel-Nolan, A. 2005. *What I like about me!* Reader's Digest Children's Books.

Sleeping Problems

Parents

Walker, M. 2018. *Why we sleep: Unlocking the power of sleep and dreams*. Scribner.

Weissbluth, M. 2015. *Healthy sleep habits, happy child, 4th edition: A step-by-step program for a good night's sleep*. Ballantine Books.

Children

Bell, A. and Naidoo, S. 2017. *The quest for rest – Polly & Pickles: An innovative two-part sleep guide that empowers and educates*. Paper Clouds Project Ltd.

Huebner, D. 2008. *What to do when you dread your bed: A kid's guide to overcoming problems with sleep*. Magination Press.

Index